ETHNIC NEEDLECRAFTS

ETHNIC NEEDLECRAFTS

By

Dr. Gauri Goel

Assistant Professor & Head

Dept. of Fashion Designing & Textiles Technology

Monad University, Hapur

(Uttar Pradesh)

(India)

DISCOVERY PUBLISHING HOUSE PVT. LTD.

NEW DELHI-110 002

Published by:
Tilak Wasan

DISCOVERY PUBLISHING HOUSE PVT. LTD.
4383/4B, Ansari Road, Darya Ganj
New Delhi-110 002 (India)
Phone : +91-11-23279245, 43596064-65
Fax : +91-11-23253475
E-mail : discoverypublishinghouse@gmail.com
sales@discoverypublishinggroup.com
parul.wasan@gmail.com
web : www.discoverypublishinggroup.com

***First Edition:* 2013**

ISBN: 978-93-5056-356-4

Ethnic Needlecrafts

Printed at:
Dynamic Printers
Delhi

Preface

India is world famous for producing a wide range of handcrafted textiles with exclusive textures and designs. Embroidery is a beautiful threadwork done on variety of fabrics, making the fabric surface more elegant and appears gorgeous.

Folk embroidery has always been a form of self expression for natives of a country. It mirrors their love and expression for nature, reflect their hidden desires and aspirations, patience and perseverance in making beautiful things. Each Indian state is unique in its textile heritage. This is mainly due to the differences in the mode of people, the availability of indigenous raw material, ecology of the place, their customs, festivals, deity, occupation, skills, likes and flare for various designing techniques.

Different hand embroideries are performed by traditional artists who are skilled in their craftsmanship and have inherited the art of embroidery from their ancestors. Today, classic embroideries viz., Kantha of Bengal, Kashida of Bihar, Kutch and Kathiawar embroidery of Gujarat, Chamba Rumal of Himachal Pradesh, Kasuti of Karnataka, Kashida of Kashmir, Embroidery of Manipur, Applique craft of Orissa, Phulkari of Punjab etc. are practiced by people of different castes and classes, particularly in the rural India.

Fashion is vicious circle; it keeps on revolving its trend from time to time, place to place and people to people, where in traditional craft always has an important role to play.

Conventional patterns, colours and stitchery provides classic platform to fashion and applied in many contemporary forms, time to time. Their gracious look and expression always attract the people demanding high fashion.

This historical view of traditional embroideries is intended to help readers navigate an array of textile issues, crossing cultural and chronological boundaries. Such embroidery history courses are very helpful for a wide variety of programs like fashion designing degree and diploma programs, textile programs with both industrial and artistic focuses, interior design programs, history, home-science degree programs and fine arts. History is a great source of inspiration, and keeping the ultimate significance of folk embroideries in mind; "Ethnic Needlecrafts" has been designed to touch on many great aspects of these textiles. This book will serve as a basic text book for some courses as well as will help to find supplement material to meet specific needs of some other courses; wherever the subject of Indian ethnic embroidery is in context.

—Gauri Goel

Contents

CHAPTER 1

Introduction

India has a rich and diverse textile heritage, where each region has its own unique fabrics and traditional attire. Traditional Indian fabrics are popular for its colourfulness and grace. The uniqueness of Indian culture lies in its geographical diversities, natural wealth, vast population and people's attitude.

Indian Needlecraft: the needle crafted fabrics includes both embroidered and appliqué technique of fabric decoration. Embroidery is the embellishment of cloth with designs made by needle and thread while Applique' or patch work refers to an art form of superimposing patches of coloured fabrics on a basic fabric/cloth to give it an altogether a new look.

Indian embroidery represents Indian culture. In India, different hand embroideries are performed by traditional artists who are skilled in their craftsmanship and have inherited the art of embroidery from their ancestors. Over the centuries, embroidery has been used to adorn everything from handkerchiefs to the most luxurious Indian attires. Embroidery adds grace and elegance, life and style even into articles of everyday use. Embroidery is an expression of self, rendered with patience and dedicated hard work, it is an art rightly described as "painting by needle". The art of hand embroidery is a painstaking and laborious process.

Characteristics of Indian Needlecraft

Regional Embroidery: embroideries of India include dozens embroidery styles varying by region to region. Different regional embroideries of India includes Kashida from Jammu & Kashmir, Chamba rumal from Himachal Pradesh, Phulkari from Panjab, Gota Kinari from Rajsthan, Various embroideries from Gujrat, Kasuti from Karnatka, Toda embroidery from Tamil Nadu, Chikankari from Uttar Pradesh and many more!

Natural Raw Material: the use of natural fibres and natural colours distinguishes the work done in India from the others. Embroidery in India is widely done on woven cloth of cotton, wool and silk; all these are sustainable.

Variety of Stitches: Indian embroidery uses many basic stitches as well as variations of basic stitches. The running stitch, back stitch, stem stitch, feather stitch, interlacing stitch, satin stitch, cross stitch etc. are just to name a few. These basic stitches and the variation of these stitches all have a unique local name in each region. The satin stitch and couching is used in Kashmir. The darn stitch produces magnificent effects in 'Bagh' and 'Phulkari' of Punjab and in 'Kantha' of Bengal. White shadow work and pulled thread work is unique to 'Chikankari' of Uttar Pradesh. Appliqué embroidery is wonderful form of Indian embroidery and is quite famous. Beaded embroidery is also the most liked form of embroidery. Shiny beads in beautiful designs impart appearance a great glow. Apart from dresses beaded embroidery also decks items like bags, footwear, fashion jewelry, household items etc. Zardozi dresses look extremely glamorous, rich and gorgeous.

Vibrant and Colourful: Indian embroidery exists in exquisite variations and vibrant colours. Embroideries from different states of India; Gujrat, Rajsthan, Kashmir, West Begal, Karnatka uses extraordinary colour combinations and create vary colourful and lively decorated fabrics. Zardozi and Banjara embroidery creates very striking effects using unique raw materials.

Naturally and Religiously Inspired Motifs: Indian embroidery takes its inspiration from nature and religion. The colours, the base, the theme and the style are reflective of a particular regions' climate and cultural background. Themes and motifs are also preservative in nature and have remained as such for centuries. The patterns have always been mainly floral, animals and religious. Each embroidery style has its own history and a story of development. Floral embroidery is one of the most popular forms of Indian embroideries. Natural beauty is highly admired by Indian people hence floral designs are all time hit in embroidery. They never cease to be in fashion and look good on everyone. Jain embroidery, Pipli craft and Pichwais are typical examples of religious embroideries of India. The motifs are specially drawn from mythological stories.

Varied uses: in India, embroidery has traditionally been used to decorate a wide variety of products like clothing and many other articles used in day to day life such as home furnishing, bags, purses, animal drapes, temple decorations, wall hangings etc. Embroidery embellishes dresses to a greater degree and makes them look appealing. Indian women opt for embroidered dresses like saree, *lehenga, choli, odhni* and children clothing.

Significance of Indian Needlecraft

Indian needlecraft includes those embroidered and appliquéd fabrics which are produced by hands with the help of simple tools like needle, frames, *aari, addas* etc. These textile products can be utilitarian, aesthetic, artistic, creative, culturally attached, religiously and socially symbolic and significant. These needle crafted fabrics plays vast role in all aspects of their life.

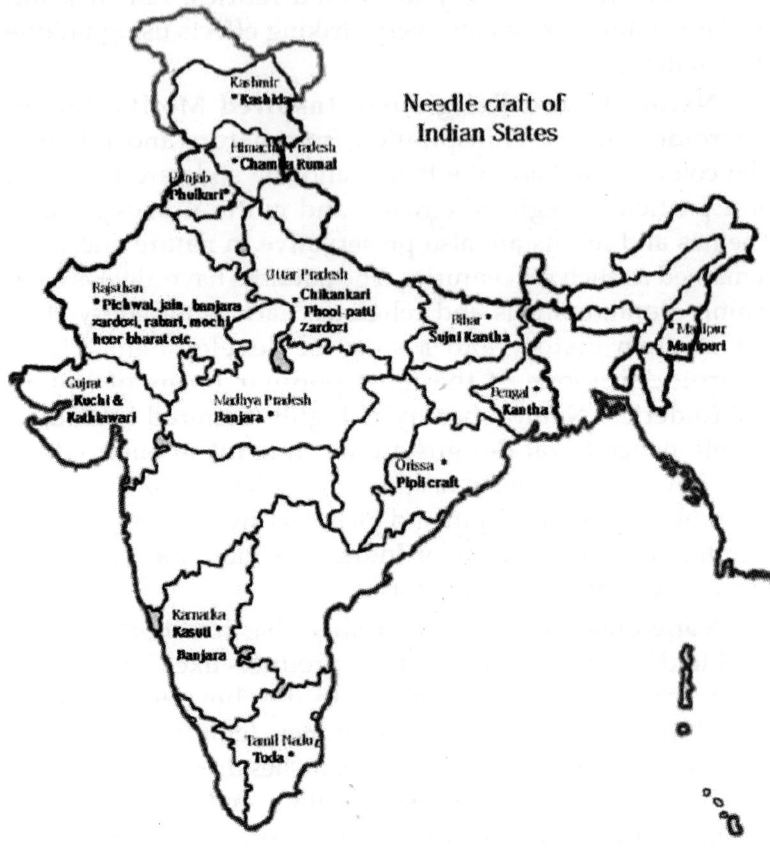

Means of Self Expression: embroidered and appliqué fabrics of India provides unique way of self expressions to the people engaged in this work. Rural and socially restricted Indian women embroider their dreams, desires, thoughts, values and culture in those beautiful fabrics.

Cultural Role: Indian needlecraft play very important role in representing the culture and traditions of the country or region. Varied embroidered textiles are a substantial medium to preserve of rich traditional art, culture, traditional skills and talents which are associated with people's lifestyle and history.

Social and Religious Role: crafts have been an integral part of village life in India. The needle lore in India helps in the growth and development of societal elements. Traditional folk techniques are passed from generation to generation. It creates a social bond between the members of a community by sharing similar art, processes and values used during embroidering fabrics. Embroidered clothing is also considered to be a symbol of living pattern, social beliefs, and artifacts of the society. Different embroidered fabrics play significant role in social and religious rituals like marriage, child birth, funeral, worships, holy festivals; holy rides of gods and goddess, temple decoration etc. Religious embroidery held great importance in India because it is a land of many religions. Dress adorned with religious embroidery is considered auspicious and is worn in religious activities and occasions.

Artistic Role: needle crafted fabrics serve the best way to display the creative and artistic skill to the people. Indian people best utilizes their leisure time in doing needle work.

Economic Significance: India is one of the important suppliers of textile handcrafted fabrics to the world market. Textile handicrafts become a prominent medium for foreign earnings. The Indian textile handicrafts industry is highly labor intensive and decentralized industry. Numerous artisans are engaged in needlecrafts' work on fulltime or part-time basis. Many agricultural and pastoral communities depend on their traditional craft skills as a secondary source of income in times of drought, lean harvests, floods or famine. Their skills in embroidery, patchwork and weaving are a natural means to social and financial independence. So it is important that these industries be more and more developed so that it is better for the people engaged in it and also for the balance in the economy of the country.

CHAPTER 2

Kashida of Kashmir

The northern most state of India, Jammu & Kashmir is famous for its natural beauty and is known as "paradise on earth". Kashmiri embroidery is colourful and beautiful as Kashmir itself. Embroidered fabrics of Kashmir, especially shawls are world famous for their rich and intricate embroidery designs. These are very expensive due to their fineness and warmth also. These embroidered shawls are such beautiful that Kashmir has become synonymous with shawls all over the world. The elegant famous Kashmiri embroidery is known as 'Kasheeda'. Kasheeda artists are very much inspired by the beauty of the nature which they have successfully reproducing in their embroidery with such an amazing skill.

The craftsmen, in Kashmir, are generally men who actually do the embroidery. The art of embroidery is kept alive by passing on this technique to future generations. The bushes of fruits, foliage and birds of brilliant hues and innumerable shades of colours are charming compounds of Kashmiri kasheeda embroidery.

Story of Kashmiri Kashida

The hand woven and embroidered shawls of Kashmir are world famous for their beauty and warmth. Dr. Abdual

Ahad, a historian from Shri Nagar, expressed that shawl weaving in Kashmir was known as early as third century B.C.

But the demand for Kashmir shawls increased during Mughal rule. The shawl industry in Kashmir was flourished by Sultan Zain-ul-abidin during 15th century. He brought craftsmen from Persia to revive the existing art. The foreign craft traditions fused together with the indigenous craft practices in Kashmir crafts. For example, the *chinar* (oriental plane), *sarav* (cypress), *sosan* (iris), *pamposh* (lotus) and the *dainposh* (pomegranate) motifs recur throughout the range of crafts.

It is evident from "Ain-e-Akbari" written by Abdul Fazal that Akbar was a keen admirer of shawls and introduced twin shawls called *'doushala'*. The demand of shawls increased in 18th century especially in European countries. It is also believed that Khwaja Yusuf during his stay in Kashmir got the idea of producing shawls with help of *'rafoogar'*. These were later known as "Amli Shawls". Amli shawls were plain woven shawls, which were ornamented with needle wholly.

Fabric: due to very cold climate of Kashmir, the fabric used for Kashmiri embroidery is mainly wool and some specialty hair fibres like Pashmina. Pure wool and pashmina wool made fabrics used for Kashmiri kashida are very expensive. Pashmina is one of the best quality wool obtained from *Capra hircus*, a species of wild Asian mountain goat. The fine fleece was obtained from under the rough, wooly, outer coat of the animal and from under belley portion. Some inferior grade wool was obtained from wild himalyan mountain sheep (*Ovis orientalis vignette*), the argali (*Ovis anunon*) and himalyan ibex (*Capra ibex*).

Nowadays, Kashida is widely performed on cheap wool and wool mixed cotton fabrics for economical point of view. Sometimes embroidery is also performed on cotton fabric for product diversification.

Threads: Embroidery thread employed earlier was fine quality woolen yarn. Gradually woolen yarns were replaced with rich & lustrous silk threads.

Now-a-days, cotton threads of bright colours with good colour fastness are also used abundantly. The bright, gorgeous inexpensive art silk (rayon) thread has also entered th industry by replacing the expensive silk threads.

Colours: The embroidery is comprised of wide spectr of colours in light and dark shades. Most commonly u colours for Kashmiri shawls are white (*Sufed*), green (*Zing*), purple (*Uda*), blue (*firozi*), yellow (*zard*), black (*mush*), crimson (*gulnar*) and scarlet (*kirmiz*). Earlier the embroidery yarns were locally dyed with indigenous natural colours but nowadays, all the threads used in the industry are invariably mill dyed with synthetic dye staff.

Stitches: Kashida embroidery of Kashmir is worked in several different forms/stitches used to adorn different articles. They are:

1. **Suzni or sozni:** Sozni is a form of extremely fine and delicate needlework mostly done on shawls and Kashmiri dresses. Designs are created as close as possible against the ground, and individual threads of the warp are taken up in the stitching and reinforced with smaller stitches. The work is done with single thread and forms very intricate patterns. Stem, cretan, fly and darning stitches are used in suzni work.
2. **Rezkari:** This is a form of needle embroidery similar in technique to sozni but the stitches are little longer and are not reinforced with additional stitches. Rezkari is done on products such as shawls, garments, table covers, and household linen.
3. **Aari-work:** It is a chain stitch done with a hooked needle called "*Aari*". The thread is passed through the needle, and is always held under the fabric to be embroidered and the hook is used to pull a series of loops, each emerging from within the previous, to the surface of the fabric.

There are two versions of this technique; the first is use to embroider on thin fabrics such as silk, wool and fine cotton cloth and is done on stoles and shawls, *Phirans* and *Poncho*, *kurta* and capes. The second is crewel work, which is done with a thicker aari and forms bolder stitches. It is mainly done on upholstery and drapery articles like cushion covers, bed covers and also on leather items. The work is mainly performed by men from the Sunni Muslim community.

4. **Kashmiri couching:** couching is also widely used technique in Kashmiri embroidery which creates very beautiful effects. Couching is done by twisting 4-6 strands of thread on the right side and couching it with a single thread of same colour. Sometimes contrasting threads are used for couching. It is a very intricate work and requires extensive training.
5. **Vata-Chikan:** this technique includes buttonhole stitch mainly used in thick fillings scenes in landscapes, gardens and crowded scene.
6. **Doria and Talaibar:** These embroidery techniques are executed with gold or silver zari (*tilla*) or silk (*dori*) thread. The work is used to embellish *pherans*, sarees and shawls. The decorative wire remains only on the surface and is secured on the cloth with a cotton thread using couching. There are two variations of the needlework in silver and metallic thread- *moraskar* (knot stitch) and *zalakadosi* (chain stitch executed in silver or metallic thread). It is used to decorate the borders of shawls and *choga*, the royal gown. The most commonly used motifs are the *pamposh* (lotus), *chinar*, *badam* (almond), *dacch-gurn* (grape leaf) and *duin* (the flower of the chinar tree).

Before commencing the embroidery work, the selected design is traced on the fabric. The perforated design sheet is placed over the fabric. Tracing is done with the help of chalk or charcoal powder. Then design is outlined with *kalam* (pen). The tracing is done by the professional tracers called *Naquashband* (*Nakshaband*) who follow the traditional technique even today. Afterward, the fabric is sent to embroiderer who finishes the design by different stitches and pressing.

Motifs: The embroidery of Kashmir is very beautiful and mainly consists of floral patterns or motifs. All the motifs are used with variation in their colours, shapes and size.

- **Flower motifs:** lilly, tulip, saffron, iris, *chinar* leaf
- **Fruits motifs:** bunches of grapes, apple blossoms, almond, cherries, plums
- **Bird's motifs:** kingfisher, parrot, wood pecker, magpie, canary

Indo-Persian Art of around 17th & 18th century provided cone shaped mango motif also known as the *kalka, badami butta* or *buta* which forms a very important motif of Kashmiri kashidakari. This motif is now produced in infinite varieties on naturalistic, geometrical and stylized designs. The *chinar* leaf motif is also most abundantly used motif along with Cyprus tree. Many beautifully coloured butterflies found in the sanctuary and Kashmir valley have also occupied an important place in the Kashida.

Animal and human figures are generally not seen in Kashmir embroidery. But few old pieces depicting hunting scenes popularly known as *Shikargah,* are available in Museums of Srinagar. The displayed pieces have embroidered borders using bands of marching soldiers and separate panels showing horse riders. The use of such motifs slowly declined.

Embroidery Terms

In Kashmir, the embroidery on shawl is done at different parts like border, corner, center and allover scattered. Different parts of the embroidered shawl are identified with different terms.

- **Hashia:** this term is used for the border design, which runs all along the length of the shawl on either side. It can be either single or double or sometimes even triple.
- **Phala:** this term is used for the embroidery done on both ends of the shawl and also called as *pallu* popularly.
- **Tanjjir or Zanjir:** border with chain stitch running either above or below the Phala.
- **Kunj Butta:** this term is used for corner design. It is usually a cluster of flowers. Butta or buta is the generic name for the floral motif specially used for conical designs. Different names are given to the design depend

upon the number of rows of buta or cones it consist: *dokad* for two rows, *sekhad* for up to five rows, *tukadar* for more than five rows.

- **Ghal:** this term is used for the decoration with embroidery in the space between the cone motifs.
- **Alifdar:** this term is used for a *Kunjabuta* that is done exclusively in green colour on white background.
- **Matanbagh:** this term is used when floral sprays are present in the entire article.
- **Jall:** all over embroidery designs are worked in trellis pattern.
- **Skikargah:** these are embroidered hunting scenes.

Embroidered Textiles from Kashmir

Kashmir is world famous for its embroidered shawls. The raw material used in Kashmiri shawls are wool, Pashmina and Shahtoosh fibers. Woolen shawls of Kashmir are being within the reach of the most modest budget, but Shahtoosh being once-in-a-lifetime purchase. A Shatush can be drawn through a ring and is, therefore, called ring shawl, and though extraordinarily light, it is nevertheless amazingly warm. Various types of woven Kashmir shawls are as follows:

Pashmina Shawl: these are superior quality pure wool shawls. They are made from wool of the Capra Hercus, a species of wild Asian mountain goat. The two grades of Pashmina are available. The first grade is the finest one named *asli-tus,* comes from wild goats and the second grade comes from the fleece of domesticated goats & mainly used in Kashmir loom industries. The most famous and finest ring shawls of mughal time were made of *asli tus.*

Doshala/Double Shawl: It is a double sided shawl. These are sold in pairs. Two identical shawls were stitched together so that when draped over shoulders wrong sides were not visible. There are many varieties of them. In the *Khali-matan* the central field is quite plain and without any ornamentation. The *Char-bagan* is made up of four pieces in different colours neatly joined together; the central part of the shawl is embellished with flowers. When the field is ornamented with flowers in the four corners, we have the *Kunj*.

Do-rookha: the *Do-rookha,* a woven shawl consists of double sided work in which there is no right & wrong side. Simple patterns are reproduced on both sides. In *doranga-dorukha,* design on one side being reproduced in another colour on the other side.

Kasaba Shawls: these are square in shape and produced on account of European demand. They are generally woven in twill and basket weave or have damask pattern against plain background.

Jamewar Shawl/ Kani Shawls: these shawls are pure wool or cotsool shawls, woven in the twill-tapestry technique and the weft threads of these shawls alone form the pattern. The fine, intricate allover paisley designs produced with silk is main characteristic of this shawl.

Amli Shawls: these are embroidered shawls with all-over embroidered designs in form of jal or hunting scenes (*shikargah*). The all-over patterns are worked in delicate fill-in stitches.

Namdas: these are embroidered rugs. The rug is a felted thick fabric manufactured by the process of pressing wool and cotton together in form of web. After that these are embroidered with thick wool in bright colours with chain stitch known as crewelwork or *Zalakdozi*. These are extensively used in Kashmiri households as an effective and inexpensive floor covering and mattress.

Gabba: It is a unique type of floor covering. In this technique, the patches of various shapes, size and colours are joined together and decorated with chain stitch. It is very cheap as old or torn woolen blankets or shawls after being washed milled and dyed in various colours are used. Embroidery is bold and vivid in designing and done with woolen or cotton threads. It is used extensively in Kashmiri households as an effective and inexpensive floor covering and is also used as a mattress in colder areas of the state.

Tapestry Work: this is also a variety of Kashmir embroidery, but in reality it is a weaving technique. It is used to make household articles and floor coverings. It is done with a blunt tapestry needle on canvas material. Designs are made with woolen threads using whip stitch. It is very laborious work.

Embroidered Garments: *Phirans, choga, angrakhas, kasaba, kurti, sherwani, poncho* etc. are the traditional costumes of people of Kashmir on which embroidery is done vigorously. *Phiran* is worn by men and women both. *Phirans* of women have intricate embroidery patterns on neckline and sleeve hem whereas *Phirans* for men are more subtle.

VARIOUS BORDER DESIGNS USED IN KASHMIRI EMBROIDERY

Suzni Style Kashmiri Embroidery

Crewel Work Border

Kashmiri Couching and Suzni Style

Floral Border Design

Traditional Border Designs in Suzni & Crewel Style

Stylized Peacock Motifs

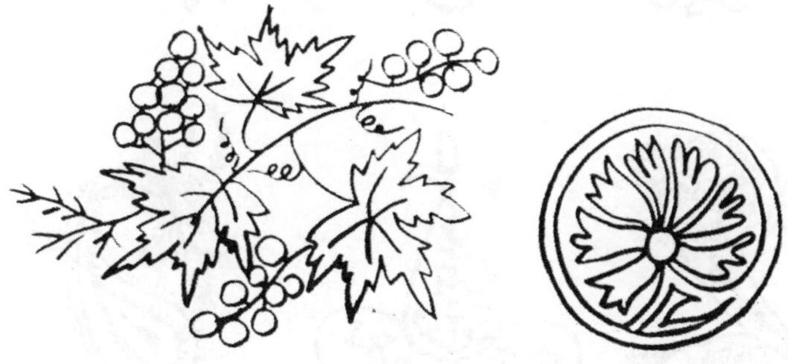

Traditional Leaf Motifs

DIFFERENT TYPES OF KALKA MOTIFS (MANGO MOTIF)

Chinar Buti

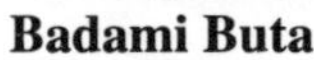

Badami Buta

Persian Style Flower

Floral Motifs

Overall Designs

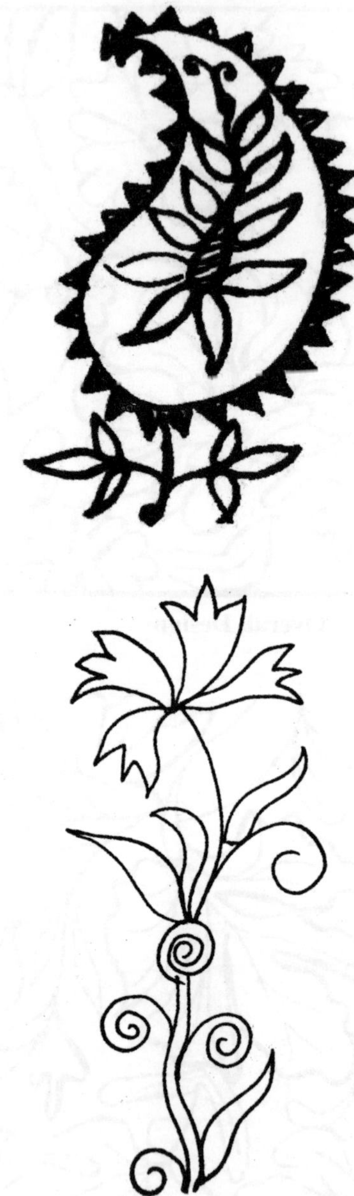

CHAPTER 3

Chamba Rumal of Himachal Pradesh

Very pictorial and striking indeed are the Rumal of Chamba, which are silk embroidered square pieces of *mulmul* used to cover dishes of food, gifts to significant persons and offerings to a deity, traditionally. Some people suggest them as small head shawls. The Chamba rumal, a form of embroidery, is practiced by ladies of Chamba. It is practiced in different parts of Himachal Pradesh like Chamba, Kulu, Kangra, Guler, Mandi and Suket. Chamba, the north-western district of Himachal Pradesh is main center for this craft. Although practiced by women from all strata of Pahari society, the embroidery style was developed by the women of the upper classes and the royalty. Chamba also has a rich history of many other crafts including metal crafts, miniature paintings, weaving, leather work, wood carving, basketry and jewelry making.

Story of Chamba Rumal

History reveals that the state of Himachal was ruled by the brave and chivalrous *Ranas* and *Thakurs*. During this era, the influence of Hinduism and poems of grate Sant Tulsidas, Kabirdas and Jayadeva, gave birth to a new form of art or Kangra style paintings. There are evidences that this luxurious embroidery is also inspired by the same and was also called as the 'Needle miniatures of Himachal' or 'Pahari rumals' during the eleventh and the twelfth century A.D.

The Chamba embroidery is believed to be flourished in the eighteenth and early twentieth century in the mountain region of north India. The history of the Chamba rumal is linked with the rulers of Chamba. After the death of the Mughal Emperor Aurungzeb in 1707, the Mughal court went into decline. The Chamba king Raja Umed Singh (1748-1768) then offered patronage to miniature artists from the Mughal courts. This patronage continued under Umed Singh's successors Raj Singh (1764-1794) and Charat Singh (1794-1808). Even before the migration of the artists from the Mughal court, Chamba was not unfamiliar with miniature painting.

Fabric: Traditionally, the fabric used to make the Chamba rumal was hand-spun or hand-woven unbleached thin muslin or *malmal*. Khaddar fabric was also used sometimes. Currently, raw materials being used are cotton, *mulmul*, silk, and polyester mixed fabrics. Tassar silk was also used in white and cream shades. Although the basic material is usually white or cream, the embroidery is invariably vivid in contrasting colour harmonies.

Threads and Colour: The threads used for embroidery was untwist silken yarn *"pat"* which gave rich effect against dull cotton ground. It produces an impression of smooth, glossy, gorgeous surface enrichment. This untwisted silk thread - usually made in Sialkot, Amritsar, and Ludhiana - was the same as that used in the Phulkari embroidery of the Punjab. Now-a-days, both twisted and untwisted yarn is being used to do the embroidery. *Gopis* were seen in vivid colours of yellow, green, dark pink and crimson combination. The outline of the figure is always worked with black.

The folk style made generous use of brilliant colours including pink, lemon yellow, purple and green while the court form evolved a more sophisticated colour palette that consisted of pale shades of ochre, dark green and blue.

Stitch: The embroidery is usually carried out with a double satin stitch *"do-rukha"*. The stitch is carried both backward and forward and covers both sides of the cloth, effecting a smooth finish that is flat and looks like colours filled into a miniature painting.

The embroidered *rumal* can be viewed from both sides, thus becomes reversible. It is done so finely that it is difficult to identify the right side, since the work is never started with a knot and the thread never been joined by knot. A simple stem-stitch using black silk thread is used to outline the figures. Other stitches like the cross stitch, the button-hole stitch, the long and short stitch, and the herring-bone stitch, as well as pattern darning, were also used occasionally.

Motifs: This *rumal* had the base of creamy white colour, on which beautiful human figures, ever green trees with colour blossoms, animals like goat and deer, saddled horse were embroidered. The traditional Chamba rumal is mainly embroidered in a square format.

The court style mainly reflects the popular pastimes of Pahari men and women from royal and noble families through the addition of details such as the smoking of the hookah, women shown talking to parrots, playing with a ball or dice or listening to music. It also derived its compositions, border motifs and floral ornamentation from the wall paintings of the *Rang-mahal* of Chamba and the Pahari miniature tradition. Often, trained miniature painters from the courts were called in to draw the compositions onto the fabric and to provide colour schemes. It is due to this close relationship with the painting tradition that the Chamba rumals have been called 'Paintings in Embroidery'.

In Pahari embroidery, the themes are taken from Purana, Ramayana & Mahabharatha. Motifs consists of symbolic animals like leaping tigers, running goats, cantering horses, jumping deer, cows, calves, birds motifs, comprised of peacock, and parrots. A range of everyday scenes, from court scenes and royal hunts, to depictions of the popular dice game of *chaupad* can be found on the rumals. Wedding processions are also depicted.

Rumal comprised of oval frame work having two or three inches of floral bodies, on all the four sides, centre of rumal has creeper motif and *guldasta* in the corners. Sometimes complete rumal has the motifs of animals, birds, trees, creepers. It is also observed that many musical instruments such as flute, *tambura*, drums, *veena*, sitar, *tabla* are depicted in the art.

Main themes in the embroidery are:

1. **Rasmandala** : depiction of dance in relation to Krishna and devotees
2. **Godhuli:** the hour of cow dust, with Krishna and his cow-herd friends bringing home the cows
3. **Kaliya damana**: Krishna killing the horrified Kalinga *sarpa*
4. **Rukmini harna**: the elopement of Rukmini and her marriage is the zist of the theme.
5. **Samundra manthana**: the ocean was churned by *devas* (Gods)
6. **Battle of kurukshetra**: *pandavas* occupy the left hand side of the panel along with lord Krishna on his chariot, *kauravas* on the right hand side and Abhimanyu is placed in centre of the panel, showing the picture of being caught in the *chakravihu*. A rumal depicting the battle of Kurukshetra is to be found at the Victoria and Albert Museum in London. This oblong piece is supposed to have been presented by Raja Gopal Singh of Chamba to the British in 1833.
7. **Raga ragini**: raga, the tune of song and ragni, the mode of song expressing the base for songs sung in a minimum of six versions.
8. **Ashta nayika**: It expresses various moods and personality of *Nayak* and *Naika*. Chamba rumals are versatile in their utility, used as a cover while offering gifts in the *mandir* (temple), either to deity or priest. Rumals were also used to cover the gifts that were exchanged during weddings.

End Uses: Men drape these colourful embroidered rumals over their shoulders and women use them as flowing veils.

The *rumal* was also used to cover gifts being exchanged between the families of the bride and groom; to cover offerings to gods during religious ceremonies and rituals; and as decorative covers, *pankhi* (hand fan) and dice boards. Today, Chamba rumal are also used as wall-hangings, door screens, cushion covers, table-cloth and bed-spreads.

Lord Vishnu Sitting on Lotus Flower

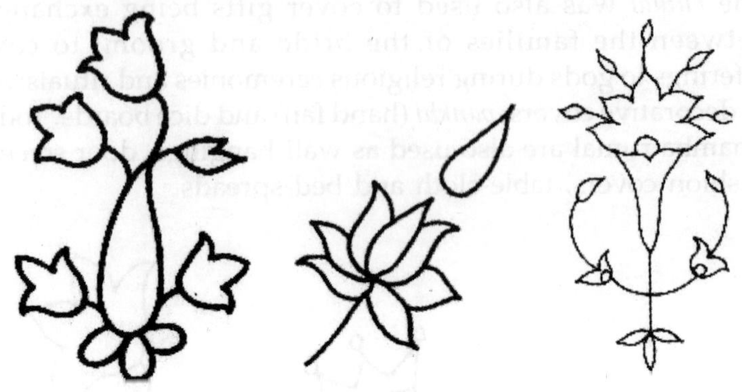

Border Motif

Prancing Deer

Lord Vishnu as Krishna with Gopis

Gopi with Dholak

Border Motif

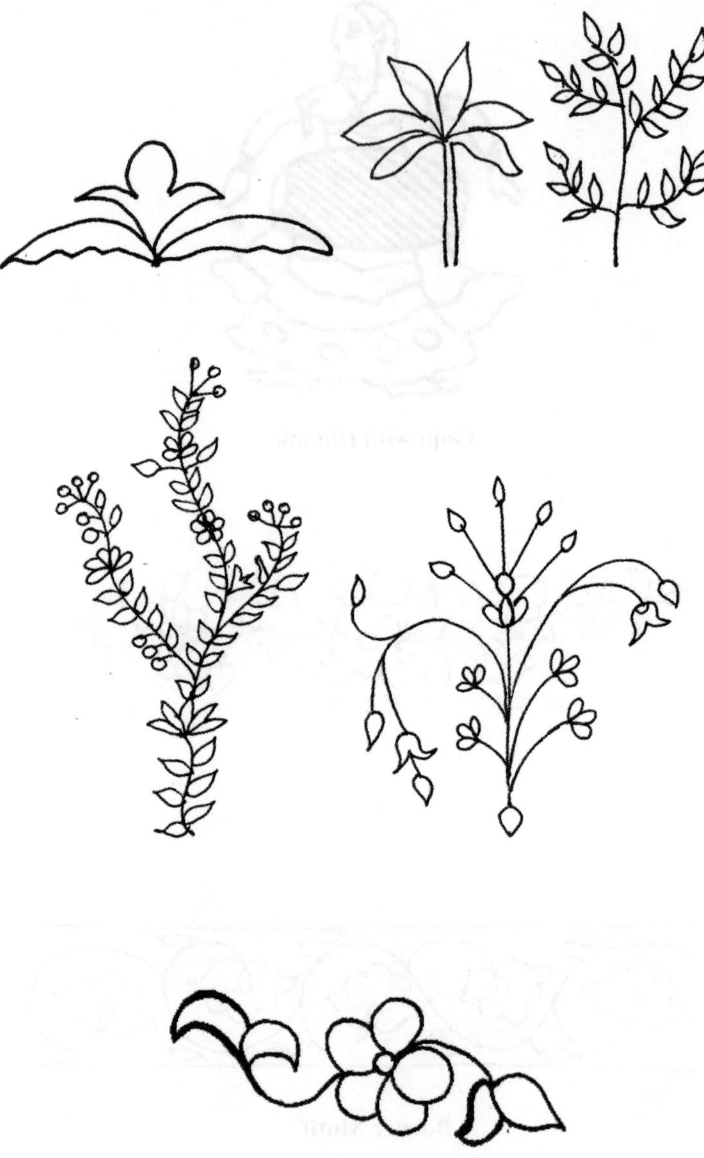

Floral Motifs

Border Design

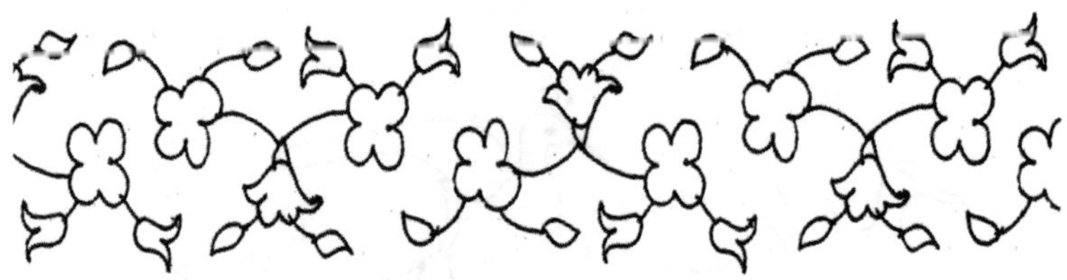

Border Design

CHAPTER 4

Phulkari and Bagh of Punjab

The phulkari and bagh are the traditional embroidered textiles from Punjab. Phulkari means 'flower craft' while Bagh means 'garden'. Phulkari work is one of the most fascinating expressions of the Punjabi folk art. It is done by the female members of a family. Women have developed this art at the cost of some of their very precious moments of leisure. It has also been customary for parents and relatives to give hand-embroidered clothes to girls in dowry. Phulkari is an integral part of the life of Punjabi girl. In any function, festival, get-together; one or the other type of phulkari or bagh is invariably used. It is believed to be auspicious, a symbol of happiness, prosperity and *suhag* of a married woman. The rough and coarse base material of phulkari symbolizes hard and tough yet colourful life of Punjabi women; the rich and glossy work with pat portrays her dreams and aspirations.

Story of Phulkari

The origin of phulkari is not quite fully known. Some say that the art was brought by Gujjar nomads from Central Asia whereas some assert that the Muslim Persians who settled in Kashmir are responsible for it. It may have some association with *Gulkari* of Persia which was practiced there. It is also said that the jats, the strongest clan in South-east Punjab who are agriculturists, introduced the art of phulkari wherever they went. The peasant women of Hissar, Rohtak, (now in Haryana), Amritser, Jhelam, Rawalpindi, Ambala, Jalandhar and Karnal are known for embroidering the best phulkaris.

Fabric: hand spun and hand woven fabric of Khaddar is the base material of embroidery of Punjab. Thread was manually spinned, loomed and dyed with natural colours. A finer khaddar fabric called as *chaunsa* is used for embroidery of Bagh. Its quality was evaluated according to the fineness and regularity of its surface. The complete khaddar for phulkari was always made of two or three stripes which were approximately fifty centimeters wide. Depending on the region, these stripes were sewed before or after the embroidery work. In West Punjab, 2 or 3 pieces of cloth are first folded and joined together. In East Punjab, they are joined together first and then embroidered.

The khaddar fabric is dyed in red, blue, and black colours. Different colour of base fabric is used for different purpose. White base fabric is also used for some phulkari work. Red was associated with youth while white Khaddar being given to mature women or widows. Black and blue colours were kept for everyday worn shawls as they prevented from revealing stains and dirt. Black and blue are not preferred in Western Punjab, whereas white is not used in East Punjab.

Thread: soft, untwisted, silk floss called *Pat* is used for embroidery work. The colours prominently used are white, golden yellow, orange, crimson, deep blue and green. Golden yellow is the most commonly used colour. Silk thread for phulkari was basically supplied from Kashmir, Afghanistan and Bengal.

It is believed that *Pat* of red-colour was used to symbolize passion, white for purity, golden or yellow for desire and abundance, green for nature and fertility, blue for serenity, purple for a symbiosis between red's energy and blue's calm, orange for a mix of desire and divine energy.

Stitches: most phulkaris are worked with the darning stitch, placed at different angles – vertical, horizontal and diagonal. The long floats of darning stitch on surface, allow large surfaces to be densely embroidered with economy. Light falling on the glossy, single colour silk threads makes the embroidery appear multi-hued. The embroidery is worked from the reverse of the fabric by the careful counting of threads, without any pattern being traced on the cloth. In order to create an unusual design or to border the khaddar, some other stitches like the herringbone stitch, running stitch and buttonhole stitch were occasionally used. Satin stitch is used on phulkari borders and blanket stitch or buttonhole stitch for finishing the edges. Occasionally, small pieces of mirrors are embroidered into the phulkari for a decorative look.

As a rule, the ornamental motifs of the phulkari are geometrical, made up of vertical, horizontal and diagonal stitches; but the bagh has an overall geometrically conventionalized floral pattern, known by various names. The darning stitch is the basic unit of phulkari and the workmanship of both bagh and phulkari are graded according to its length and density of stitches.

Motifs: the most common motifs for phulkari include geometrical flower motifs inspired by nature, as the name itself suggests. Images of flowers and vegetables, wheat and barley stalks, the sun, the moon, trees and rivers, Mughal gardens, kites and even playing- cards were stitched on phulkaris and baghs. Motifs from daily life, houses, temples, animals and wedding rituals were also represented in work from east Punjab.

The result of phulkari embroidery is inevitably dazzling with bright, lustrous coloured threads shining on a red background. But, on close inspection, one may find **Nazar buti**, a small unfinished area or a patch with a different pattern, setting it apart from the rest of the piece. The embroiderer introduces this apparent imperfection, to keep off the evil eye that may cast itself on a beautiful piece of work, and the wearer.

There are many kinds of phulkari and bagh, and are listed below:

Types of Phulkari

1. **Chope:** the chope is usually presented to the bride by her grandmother during a ceremony before the wedding. The bride's maternal grandmother starts chope's embroidery as soon as her granddaughter born. Chope is bigger than other phulkari. Its khaddar was invariably dyed in red or orange colour, symbol of passion and happiness. It is worth noticing that chope was never bordered so that this happiness could be unlimited. Pat was always chosen in golden tones to express desire and wealth. The Patterns were big triangles symmetrically distributed on the two sides of the chope's longitudinal axis.
2. **Suber or Subhar:** suber is another rich and gorgeous, Phulkari worn by the bride when she walks around the sacred fire during her wedding. This is also made on red coloured fabric with "silk pat". Suber has one central eight-petalled lotus motif and four corner motifs. The central motif is repeated on corners.
3. **Tilpatra:** tilpatra literally means dotted with "til seed" (sesame seeds) designs. It has small embroidery dots or buties in the body of any inferior and inexpensive khaddar. It is presented to the maids during wedding and other traditional auspicious occasions.
4. **Nilak:** nilak is the black or navy blue coloured khaddar shawl, embroidered with yellow or crimson red *pat*. This is very popular among the present women. The motifs commonly embroidered are the articles used at household like comb, fan, umbrella and flowers.
5. **Saloo:** this is the red or black coloured shawl meant for daily use. Simple phulkari embroidery is done on it with a single colour.

6. **Shishedar Phulkari:** the tiny mirror pieces are embroidered in the shawls. The ground colour is red or chocolate-brown and the embroidery is in yellow or slate blue silk.
7. **Surajmukhi:** surajmujkhi, the sunflower, refers to the main pattern of this phulkari.
8. **Darshana Dwar or Darwaza:** darshan dwar, that can be translated as "the gate through which God can be seen", unlike other phulkari was not made for a person but for a temple as an offering to thank the gods after a wish had been fulfilled. It is a unidirectional design worked on a panel of red colour. These profusely embroidered textiles bear human figures standing at the portals of the shrine, along with other motifs.
9. **Thirma:** it is a phulkari done on white khaddar. It is specialty of Hindu women from the north of Punjab. As a symbol of purity, thirma was often worn by elder women but, at times, this choice of white coloured khaddar was also made for esthetical reasons. The *pat* was generally chosen in a range of bright pink to deep red tones. Cluster stitched flowers, wide triangles covering the forehead as well as chevron darning stitch surfaces were very common thirma patterns.
10. **Sainchi Phulkari:** It is the folk embroidery of Malva region of Punjab depicts the true rural life. The motifs depict the various activities of rural life like ploughing, harvesting, a water carrier, and smoking *hukka*, pounding, grinding, churning, spinning and weaving and so on. Local animals like goats, cows, elephants, big cats, scorpions, peacocks are also represented. In addition, they were produced in a relatively small area (Firozpur and Bhatinda districts) and required high embroidery skills. These are all the reasons why they became so appreciated by collectors and occupy a very unique position among the different varieties of phulkari.

Bagh

When the embroidery work was covering the whole surface of the khaddar, the phulkari was called a bagh ("garden"). Embroidery is so profuse that the ground colour is no longer visible. The making of a bagh was requiring so much talent and patience (sometimes more than a year) that it was kept for very special occasions. Furthermore, the quantity of *pat* needed to achieve such a piece was implying big expenses and thus was a way for families to display their wealth. Bagh fabric has all over geometrical motifs. The whole background is embroidred with two colours of *pat* like white and yellow, orange and yellow or green and crimson etc.

1. **Ghunghat Bagh:** Ghunghat bagh is a shawl used by bride as a veil to cover face. Embroidery is done on the triangular patch which covers the face. Embroidery is done mainly with golden yellow colour on red back ground. Multi colour threads are also used to decorate the shawl.
2. **Vari da Bagh:** It is a bagh given to the bride from groom's side. It is made by grandmother of the groom, and is very elaborately embroidered. Vari-da-bagh is always made on an orange-reddish khaddar and, except for its border and sometimes a small decoration, it is always embroidered on its whole surface with a single golden or orange coloured pat.

   This bagh's main pattern is a group of three or four small concentric lozenges of growing size included in each other. Despite the fact that only one colour of pat is used, these lozenges are easily revealed by the reflections of light.
3. **Bawan Bagh (Bawan Phulkari):** Bawan means "fifty-two" in Punjabi and refers to the combination of fifty-two different patterns on the fabric. An interesting method of preserving motifs was expressed on the Bawan Bagh. The cloth was divided in 52 squares, each of which was filled in with a different motif. Bawan-bagh was very

important in preserving patterns. It is said that Bawan bagh is the rarest of all the bagh and phulkari.

4. **Chand Bagh:** A chand bagh derives its name from the dominant motif of large diamonds done with horizontal and vertical darning stitches. The subtle change in the directions of the stitch, its gloss and the colour are suggestive of highly stylized chands (moon).

Various other baghs are named according to the motifs embroidered on them. These baghs are: *surajmukhi* bagh, *kakri* bagh (cucumber motif), *karelian da* bagh (bitter ground motif), *mirchi* bagh (chilly motif), *dhaniya* bagh (coriander bagh), *genda* bagh (marigold motif), *zanzir da* bagh (zigzag line motif) etc. The baghs are also named according to the number of colours used like: *dwiranga* (two-colours), *panchranga* (five-colours), *satranga* (seven-colours), *navranga* (nine-colours) etc. *Tota* bagh (parrot motif), *mor* bagh (peacock motif), *Shalimar* bagh and *dhup-chaon* bagh (shaded effect) are some other famous types of baghs.

Products: Once done to be gifted to brides, and never for commercial sale, phulkari embroidery is now worked on varieties of home and commercial products like curtains, bedspreads, cushion covers, wall hangings, chiffon sarees, *kurtas* or shirts and *dupattas* or shawls.

TRADITIONAL PHULKARI MOTIFS

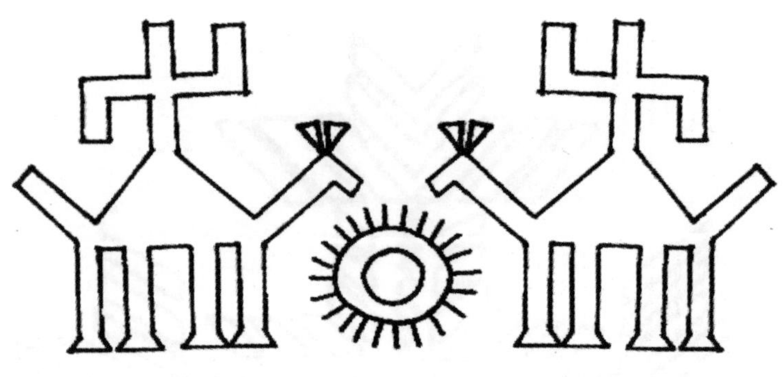

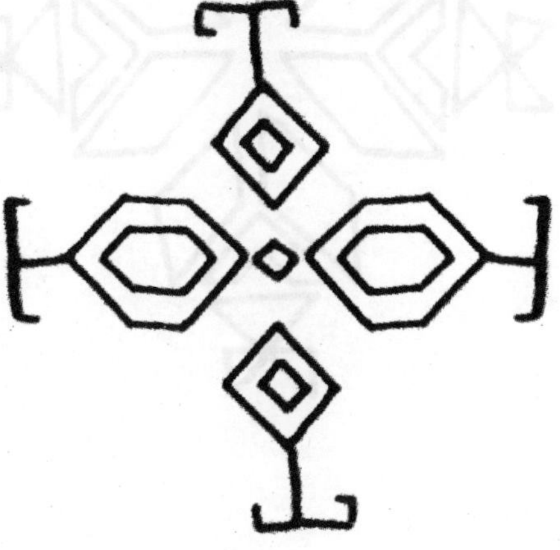

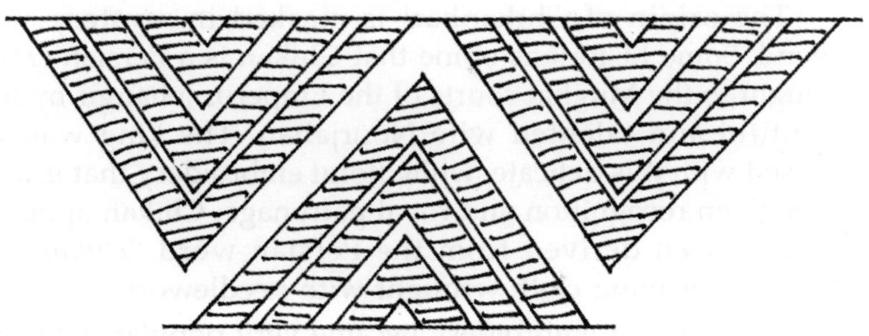

CHAPTER 5

Chikankari Embroidery of Uttar Pradesh

Chikankari is the famous needlecraft of Lucknow, Uttar Pradesh. Chikan Embroidery has a unique grace and elegance which can be produced only with a single colour, white-on-white. Its delicacy is mesmeric. In its contemporary form, this embroidery is also available in coloured forms. Finely detailed and dense floral patterns with knots, pulled work and other textural elements are characteristic of this work. The art of chikankari, today is flourishing and enriches both the domestic and export market.

Story of Chikankari

The origin of Chikankari is masked in mystery and legend. Some historians opine that Chikan is a Persian craft, brought to the Mughal courts of the Emperor Jehangir by his beautiful and talented wife Noorjahan. The king was so pleased with this delicate, white floral embroidery that it was soon given recognition and royal patronage. Chikan appears to have been derived from the Persian word *"chikin"* or *"chakin"*, meaning cloth wrought with needlework.

This form of embroidery became very popular with the king and his nobles and was embroidered on the finest Daccai mulmuls or muslin garments which were most appropriate for the hot, tepid climate of Delhi. There are some very fine Mughal miniatures that depict the Emperor Jehangir in white flowing muslin garments believed by historians to be "chikan". After the decline and fall of the Mughal court, the artisans and craftsmen scattered across the length and breadth of India. Some settled in West Bengal, so for some time chikan flourished in Calcutta, though it is no longer practiced there. Some fled to the Northern state of Awadh and settled in the Awadh royal courts. Under the cultured, sophisticated influence of the rulers of Awadh, chikankari began to flourish.

Kamala Devi Chattopadhyaya opines that Chikan can be dated back to the time of King Harsha, who is said to have had "a great fondness for white embroidered, muslin garments. Megasthenes, dating back to the 3rd century B.C. has written of the use of 'flowered muslin' by the Indians in the court of Chandragupta Maurya.

Chikancraft gained a meaningful presence in Lucknow and its surrounding areas sometime during the late 18th and early 19th century when it was brought to the 'Lakhnawi' courts of the nawabs. It was patronized by the self-indulgent, pleasure-loving nawabs, favoured by local kings, sultans and zamindars and became a very intrinsic part of Lakhnawi grace and culture. Chikankari is also produced in Varanasi, Ducca, Bhopal, Allahabad, Calcutta and Gaya; but the best quality comes from Lucknow.

Fabric: This embroidery was traditionally done on white cotton fabric like muslin or cambric. But now it is done on variety of fabrics like crepe, organdie, *mulmul*, chiffon, georgette, muslins, voiles and net.

Thread: Originally, chikan embroidery was done with white cotton thread, bleached or unbleached. For pulled work, thread was drawn from selvedge of the fabric. Today chikan work is not only done with coloured threads but on coloured fabrics of many fibres. Traditional white thread is embroidered on cool, pastel shades of light muslin and cotton garments.

To provide a glittering look to the embroidery, beads and sequin work have now gained wide acceptance.

Motifs: In chikankari embroidery designs are mainly of scrolling floral and leaf patterns. Paisley motif is the most popular motif in chikan embroidery. In India Paisley is known as *"Kairi"* (mango motif). The design motifs in Chikankari are predominantly influenced by Mughal art. Beautiful floral *butis,* foliages, creepers and fruits are made. Border designs like *dhaniya patti* (coriander leafs) and creepers are very popular. Animal motifs are also made, which include fish, elephant and parrot.

Stitches: Chikenkari embroidery involves about forty different stitches, which can be broadly divided into 3 groups: flat stitches, embossed stitches, and the open trellis (jali work). Out of these forty stitches, six basic stitches; *taipchi, bakhia, murri, phanda, jali* and *jangira* are most commonly used.

1. **Taipchi:** It is also called as "do-ruha" and produces same effect on both sides. Taipchi is running or darning stitch worked with six strands on the right side of the fabric. This is the simplest chikan stitch and often serves as a basis for further embellishment. It is occasionally done within parallel rows to fill petals and leaves in a motif, called *"ghaspatti"*. Sometimes taipchi is used to make the *bel-buti* all over the fabric. It is considered the cheapest and the quickest stitch.
2. **Bakhia:** Bukhia consists of inverted satin stitch or herringbone stitch. It is the most common stitch and is often referred to as shadow work. It is of two types. In *"ulta Bakhia"* the floats lie on the reverse of the fabric underneath the motif. The transparent muslin becomes opaque and provides a beautiful effect of light and shade. In *"Sidhi Bakhia"* satin stitch with criss-crossing of individual threads or herringbone stitch is done. The floats of thread lie on the surface of the fabric. This is used to fill the forms and there is no shadow effect.

3. **Murri:** Murri falls under embossed knotted style of chikankari. It is a rice shaped stitch produced by minute satin stitches. Murri is worked at the centre of the flowers.
4. **Phanda:** Phanda resembles grain like the millet; this is also embossed knotted style. It is a French knot. It is a smaller shortened form of murri. The knots are spherical and very small. It is used in the centre of the flowers in ordinary chikan work motifs
5. **Gitti:** It is a combination of buttonhole and long satin stitch, usually used to make a wheel-like motif
6. **Hool:** is a fine detached eyelet stitch. A hole is punched in the fabric and the threads are teased apart. It is then held by small straight stitches all round and worked with one thread on the right side of the fabric.
7. **Jangira:** Chain stitch usually used as outlines and worked with one thread on the right side of the fabric.
8. **Rahet:** it is a stem stitch worked with six strands producing a solid line on front of fabric. It is used for outline only.
9. **Khatawa or katow:** This is similar to *bakhia*, but finer and is a form of appliqué work or cutwork, more a technique than a stitch. This belongs to flat style of chikankari work. This work is made on white calico material, and not done on fine muslin. Design (paisley and floral patterns) is prepared, placed over the surface of the final fabric and stitched on to it.
10. **Jali work:** The jalis or trellises are a unique specialty of this craft, give an effect of open mesh or net like appearance. The holes are made by manipulation of the needle without cutting or drawing of thread. The warp and weft threads of the fabric are carefully drawn apart to make neat regular holes or jalis and minute buttonhole stitches are inserted into the cloth. Shape of openings and the stitches used, distinguish one jaali from another. There are various kinds of jali, but the technique is the

same, each jali is made in different patterns. The common and popular are Bengali, *Siddaur*, Tajmahal, *Phool jali, Satkani, Tabar, Chitegul and Kanthmahal* and Madrasi jalis.

The various other types of legendary chikankari stitches are: *Pechani, Bijli, Ghaspatti, Makra, Kauri, Hathkadi, Banjkali, Sazi, Karan, Kapkapi, Madrazi, Bulbul-chasm, Taj Mahal, banarasi Kangan, Dhania- patti, Rozan, Meharki, Chanapatti, Baalda, Jora, Keel kangan, bulbul, sidhaul,* etc. Some of these have equivalents in other embroideries, the rest are manipulations that make them distinctive and unique.

Process: The pattern is engraved on a wooden blocks or sketching is done manually. Once the block is ready printing is done on the fabric. Printing is carried out by the use of wooden blocks dipped in dyes like *neel* and *safeda* to make a pattern. The printed fabric then reaches the craftsmen who work on the cloth. Fabric is stretched by a wooden frame, during embroidery process. After the embroidery, the fabric is laundered and finished for sale. The finishing process may include bleaching, stiffening and ironing.

Chikankari Products: traditionally Chickankari work was performed mainly on cap, *chapkan, angrakhas* and *kurta*. In its contemporary form it is done on garments of both male and female including female *kurtis, sarees,* stoles, male *kurta,* cap etc. Now-a-days this embroidery is also performed on various handcrafted and home furnishing items.

CHIKANKARI MOTIFS

Shadow Work Motif

Kairi (Mango) Motif

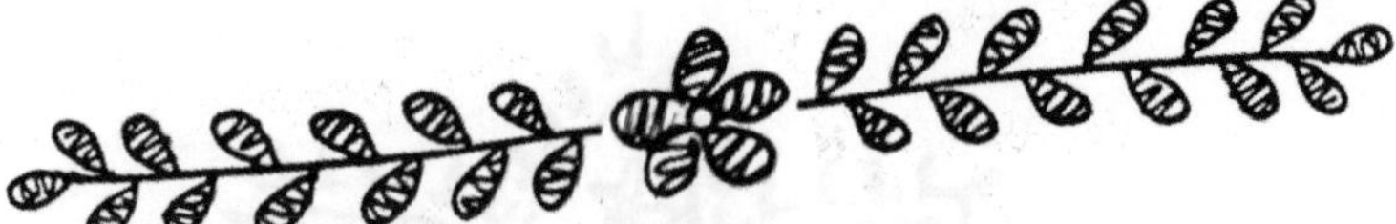

Jali Work Motif

Murri Work Motif

Fish Bel (Applique Work)

CHAPTER 6

Embroideries of Gujarat

Gujarat, the state situated in the western part of India, is famous for the embroidery of Kutch and Kathaiwar. The peasant, tribal and ladies of other community residing in the villages have maintained their tradition, culture and rich heritage through various styles of embroideries. Embroideries of Gujarat state have greatest contribution to the Indian textile heritage. The embroidery articles from Gujarat were world famous and exported to European countries during 16th and 17th century.

Marriage costumes, wall hangings, quilts, cradle cloths and animal trappings are very beautifully embroidered in different parts of Gujrat. In addition to embroidery stitches, Gujrati textiles are appliquéd, decorated with beadwork and embellished with mirrors, sequins, and shells. Each caste represents its own distinct designs, colours and range of stitches and passes their culture from generation to generation.

EMBROIDERY OF KUTCH

The Rabari shepherds, *Kanbi* farming, *Mochi* cobler and *Ahir* herding castes are the main practitioners of what can be loosely termed the *'Kutchi'* style of embroidery. The

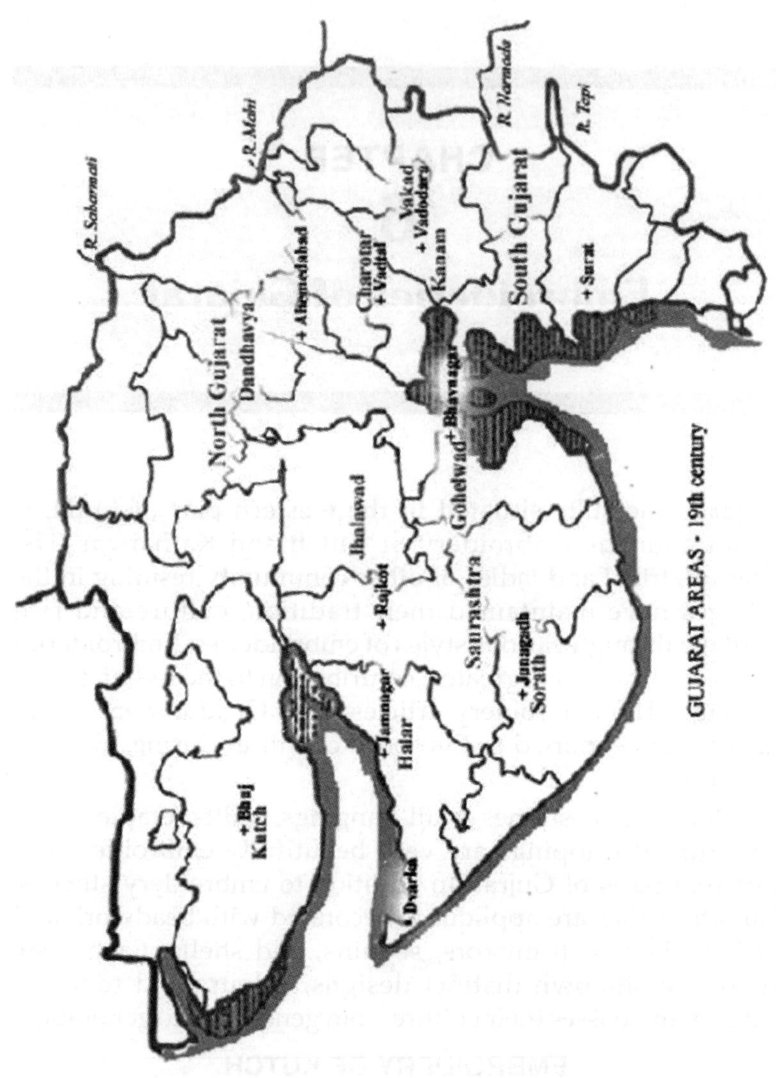

GUJARAT AREAS - 19th century

embroidery is characterized by predominant chain, herringbone and open-chain stitching and the profuse use of mirrors in the case of the *Rabari* and *Ahir*. They embroider in white, yellow, green and red and sometimes a little blue, mainly in cotton. Motifs are floral with women dancing, churning butter or carrying water pots on their heads.

Mochi/Aari Bharat Embroidery

The "aari bharat", or "Mochi bharat" is a famous needlework from Gujarat. Mochi is the community belonged to the artisan, cobbler or shoe maker in Kutch and Saurashtra. The centre for Mochi embroidery was Bhuj, the capital of Kutch, but some Mochis worked elsewhere in Kutch and other moved to Saurashtra. It is best known as arhi/aari bharat, named after a hooked needle arhi or aari. It is said that Mochi people learned their craft from a Muslim *fakir* who came from Sind two hundred and fifty years ago. Traditionally this art is associated generally with men artisans. While male artisans undertake the stitching of the objects, the women embroider them with a variety of designs.

Stitch: A hooked needle is used in the embroidery called the aari. The fabric is first fixed over the wooden frame, pattern is traced on it and the embroidery work begins. Aari work looks like a fine chain stitch. Although the technique is simple in principle, it requires extensive skills and long practice.

Fabric: The surface materials are silk, mashru (a woven cloth of one pick cotton and one pick silk), broadcloth, satin (known as *gajji*), or canvas. The embroidery is performed using twisted silk threads.

Motif: The actual embroidery is accomplished without prior design and follows the format of leaves, foliage, flowers, fruits, animals, and human figures in a chain stitch variation. Many of the design motifs indicate a Persian or Mughal influence (*butas* and peacocks) but when the Mochis immigrated to other regions, they readily adopted the prevailing design iconography of the new area.

Products: Mochi embroidery was traditionally executed on household objects. Items such as the ghagara (skirt), choli (bodice), and caps were and are often embroidered. Home furnishings include the coverlet (chakla), and door panels (toran and sthapana).

Kanbi Bharat Embroidery

Kanbi Bharat is commonly practiced by the Kanbis of Kutch. In Kanbi Bharat, Kanbis denotes the caste and Bharat denotes the embroidery. Kanbis are the group of people, migrated from Saurashtra, whose main occupation was farming. The women communities engage themselves in the beautiful art of bharat.

The Kanbi group is composed of two communities: the *Kadwas* who live in central Saurashtra and western Sorath, and the *Lewas,* who are concentrated in Bhavnagar, Gariadhar, and Kundla.

Threads: The embroidery thread is cotton of yellow, orange, green, white and purple colours.

Stitches: The basic stitches employed are darning for out lining and herring bone for filling. However the lewa *Kanbi* from Bhavnagar uses the chain stitch even though herringbone stitch may also be employed for floral designs.

Motifs: The embroidery depicts primarily birds, flowers and creepers or vines and tendrils. The specific motifs are the sunflower, kevada, cactus flower and parrots. The designs in Kanbi Bharat are distinct and have the influence of Persian art.

Articles: Animal trappings are one of the principal forms of embroidery. The articles more frequently prepared are the rectangular cover spread on the back of the bullock, conical covers, attractively tasseled to cover the horns, gorgeously embroidered veils to cover the forehead, face and muzzle. The *"jhul"* is the covering for the back of the animal, the tasseled *"shingadiyas"* or *"shingrotiyas"* covers the horns, the *"lalavati"*, *"mathavati"*, or *"matharotiyam"* adorns the forehead, the *"khobra"* is the face covering, and the muzzle is called the *"makhiyala"*.

The other household articles like covers for wooden boxes, *patras*, blankets and quilts, on which elaborate embroidery of parrots, peacocks, various shapes of foliages, climbers, creepers, tender twigs of mango are commonly observed.

Rabari Work

The rabaris are a wandering group of people who are recognized for their distinctive arts, particularly embroidery, mirrored mud sculpture and beadwork. Rabari embroidery of Gujarat is considered as the first and the foremost in the race of leading handicrafts of Gujarat. Rabari are mainly shepherds belong to a Giri region, usually migrating from place to place for their life.

Fabric: This embroidery is very effective, impressive and attractive, usually done on a handspun, hand woven khaddar or Khadi material mainly of maroon colour.

Motif: The motifs comprised of beautiful birds, flora and fauna, human figures and so on. Women balancing pots on their heads (*Paniyari*), mango leaves, scorpions, camels, parrots, elephants, flowers and the tree of life are some of the beloved and auspicious motifs of rabari embroidery.

Stitches: The stitches used are chain interlaced with buttonhole for mirror work, and chain stitch for filling purpose. Rabaris also use decorative back stitching, called *bakhiya*, to decorate the seams of women's blouses and men's *kediya* jackets.

Products: Rabaris embroider an extensive range of garments, household decorations, bags and animal trappings. Girls of Rabari community traditionally embroider skirts, veils, blouses, wall hangings, purses, pillows and *Kothalo*-the dowry sacks.

Married women adorn children's clothing as well as cradle cloths. The mirrors which are embroidered also guard their children against evil spirits that are believed to inhabit their world.

The finest rabari embroidery with most intricate patterns is created by Mutwa and Jat communities. The Mutwas, staying in Banni, embroider fabric using small mirrors and are perfect in many distinct styles. They use silk and fine handspun cotton in white, golden yellow, blue, black and red to develop patterns and booties of animal and bird motifs. The Jats, migrated from the regions of Baluchistan, are skilled in inserting even the smallest of the mirrors with extreme precision, using pleasant colours and patterns generally geometric.

Ahir Bharat

The primitive peasants of Saurashtra are known regionally as Ahirs. Later they migrated to Kutch. Ahir tribes can be found in Kutch - chiefly Bhuj, Anjar and Mandvi talukas. Their style is similar to mochi or aari embroidery. This work is also done with a hooked needle and appears exactly like chain stitch. The base material used was dark coloured hand spun and hand woven coarse khaddar. Along with embroidery from chain stitch, abundant application of mirrors is also observed. In olden days colourful cotton threads were used for embroidery but now-a-days silken threads are also used.

The ladies of ahir families embroidered their traditional costumes like blouses, choli, pajamas, caps and children clothes, during their off seasons. Sets of embroidered clothing lavishly decorated with mirrors forms an important part of their ceremonial clothing. Motifs such as peacocks, parrots, scorpions, elephants, the milk maid and flowers, tear drop shapes etc. are used.

Ganesh Hangings

Ganesh hangings are one of the most distinctive of all the folk embroideries of Gujarat. This consists an embroidered image of Lord Ganesha (the elephant -headed god) on a white background. Ganeshtapana is a pentagonal wall-hanging often with yellow background. Lord Ganesha is embroidered in the centre of the Ganeshtapana, often with his bowl of sweets and his companion rat, and almost always is set between his two wives, Siddhi and Ridhdhi. A border of flowers, birds, or animals like elephant is worked around the edge of the Ganeshtapana.

EMBROIDERY OF KATHIAWAR

The Kathiawar embroidery is very colourful, elaborate and lavish. The exquisite embroidered items form Kathiawar are:

1. **Chakla:** Chaklas are square pieces, to cover the door frame. These are carrying bold motifs of birds and animals.
2. **Chandrawar:** Chandrawas is a rectangular piece used as wall hangings and others decorative purposes.
3. **Toran:** Toran is a long embroidered piece of patterned cloth, decorating the lower edges of the pelmet.
4. **Patti:** Patties are embroidered fabric stripes, running the length of wall.
5. **Ghagra and choli:** traditional dress of Kathiawar women.

Abhala Bharat

Abhala bharat (mirror embroidery), a traditional embroidery of Kathiawar, has now become a part of the ethnic fashion all over the world. It uses small mirror discs fixed with closely worked stitches. In abhala bharat is very lively and bright colours are used and mirrors gives most striking effects to the fabric. Mirrors are attached with silken thread using chain and herringbone stitch, while the remaining background is filled by herringbone stitch. Usually, the mirror work is done on a dark background with motifs like flowers, creepers, petals, etc. traditional colours used in this embroidery are red, pink, green, yellow and blue. Abhala bharat is generally seen in *gaghras* (skirts), *cholis* (bodices), *odhnis* (shawls), bags, wall hangings, bed spreads and many other ornamental pieces for home décor.

Sindhi Taropa

This style is prevalent in the Thar and adjoining districts of Sind, in Banni Kutch and in the western Rajasthan districts of Barmer and Jaisalmer.

In Sindhi taropa embroidery is done by thread interlacing. In interlacing process firstly long stitches are taken into base fabric to form basic structure and then interlacing is done into the basic structure to form pattern. The designs consist of mainly squares, lozenge, chevron and discs. Sometimes deigns are inspired by bird, flowers and animals.

Moti Bharat

Kathiawar and Kutch places of Gujarat state are famous for beads work or Moti work. It is a specialty of Rajkot, Bhavnagar, Jamnagar, & Junagarh.

They do not use any base fabric for bead work, but by use of only colourful threads and different shapes of beads they produce exclusive articles. The colours used were mostly orange, green, yellow, purple & red. The kathi beadwork motifs portrayed divine and human figures, combined with flowers, cradles, racing camels, other animals and birds, and were worked in translucent and semi-translucent coloured beads set in a background of white opaque beads.

The popular items of beads work are cradles, purses, *indhonis* (little perches that sit on women's head to balance water pots), *pankha* (fan), *gahumri* (swastika), *chakla, toran* (door pelmets), *sogta baji* (chess game).

Banni Embroidery or Heer Bharat

The embroidered fabrics that come from Banni in Kutch are famous for bright yellow, red and saffron colours and mirror work with beads. The embroidery is done using the silk floss called heer locally. The fabric is embellished with architectural designs and is also called Heer Bharat. The embroidery is done by the Jat community and is known for the intricacy and richness. It is typical embroidery manipulating the weave of the fabric. The mirrors are studded using buttonhole and chain stitch.

Kathi Embroidery

The handicrafts of Gujarat being a prime attraction for the tourists on tour to Gujarat are really unique in their own charm and grace. Kathi Embroidery of Saurashtra is unique in its own kind, among the different embroideries of Gujarati handicrafts.

Owing its roots to the nomadic rabari tribe of Gujarat, the Kathi embroidery is the oldest form of Gujarati embroidery and mainly comprises of use of mirrors and colourful threads stitched together to give the feel of patch work. The black silk or satin fabric is mainly used. Stitches used are herringbone, darning and chain. Several kinds of intensely vivid coloured threads of scarlet, purple, yellow are used to stitch the form of Kathi embroidery and lots of appliqué work is used in this form of embroidery.

Beautiful prominent designs depicting figures of animals, birds, flowers and plants are made on the fabrics. Specifically, designs of tigers, elephants and cobras are styled on the materials as symbols of elegance and grace. Small mirrors are used as eyes of birds or flower centers. Geometrical motifs are fabricated with multi-coloured fabric pieces in patch work effect.

Soof Embroidery

Soof embroidery is done by Sodha Rajput and Harijan women who migrated from Pakistan in 1971 the during indo-pak war. It is also called "Sodha Bharat". In Rajasthan, Rabari women are also well known for this embroidery. Embroidery is somewhat similar to phulkari, done by using satin stitch by inserting the needle from behind the cloth and designs come on the front side. Triangle motifs and symmetrical patterns are characteristics of this embroidery. Soof is done by counting the warp and weft of the cloth and motifs are never drawn. The articles made are *odhani, thalposh* and waist and head bands.

Khaarek

Khaarek is also a geometric style of embroidery. It is done by counting the threads like soof. In this style, geometric patterns patterns are made and space is filled with bands of satin stitch that are worked along warp and weft of the fabric. *Khaarek* embroidery fills the entire fabric. In older *khaarek* work, cross stitching was also used.

TRADITIONAL GUJARATI MOTIFS

Design in Chain Stitch

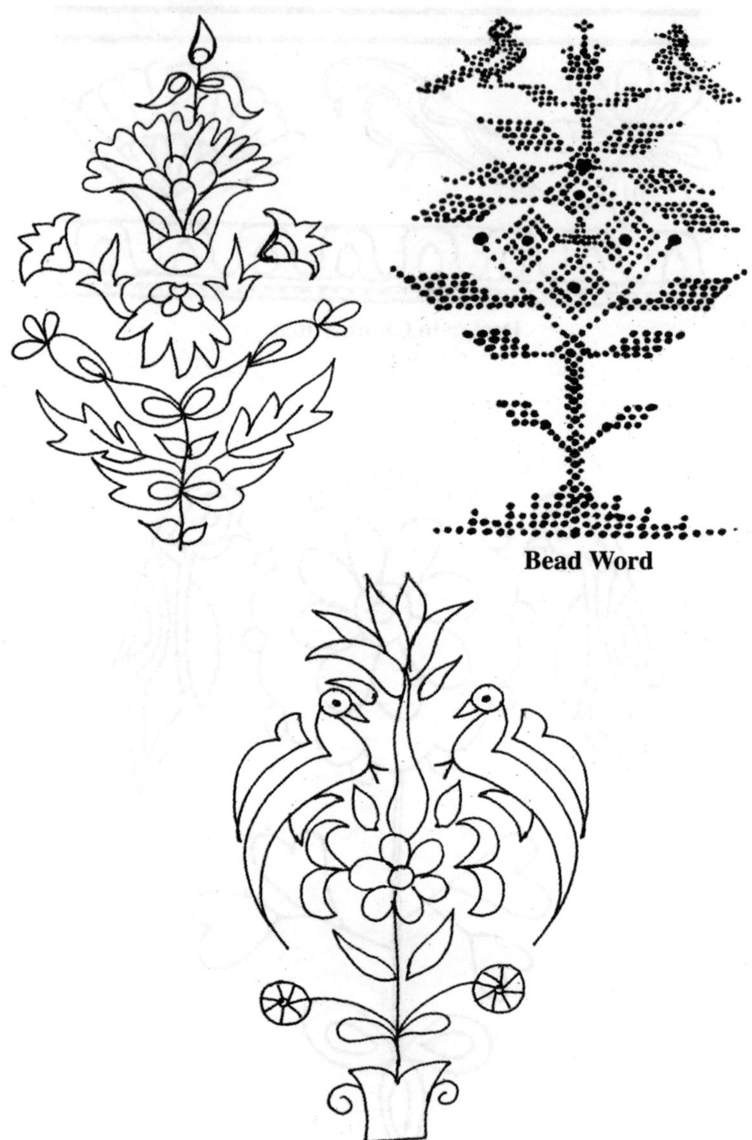

Bead Word

Bead Work Design

Border Designs

Motifs with Mirror Work

Peacock Motifs

Sindhi Taropa

Soof Embroidery Motifs

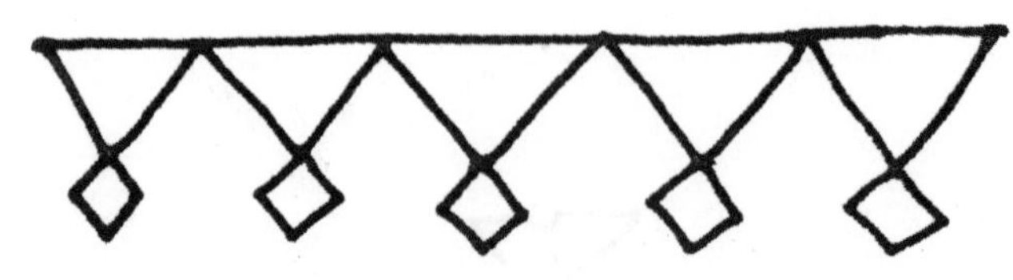

Motif to be done in Chain Stitch

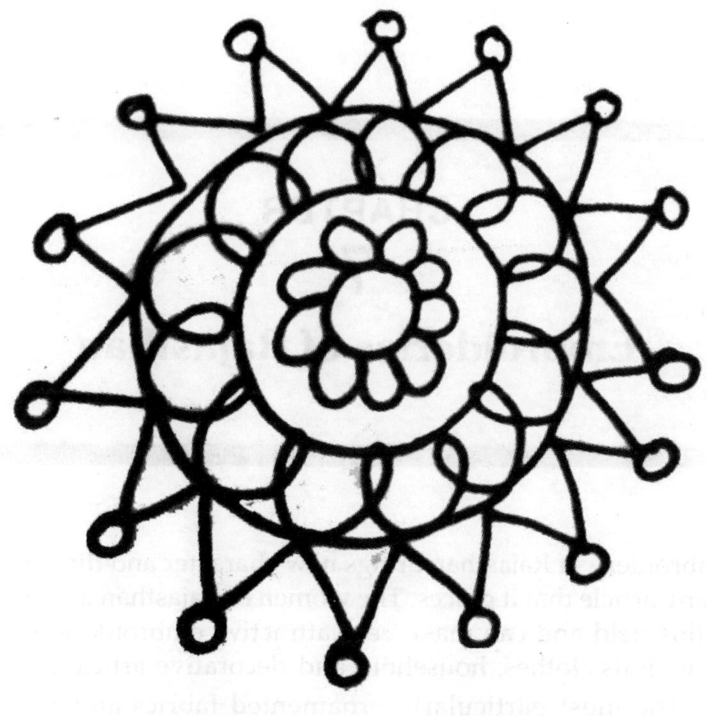

Mirror Work Motif

CHAPTER 7

Embroideries of Rajasthan

Embroidery of Rajasthan brings new character and dimension to any article that it graces. The women of Rajasthan are expert in this field and can make very attractive embroidery works on various clothes, household and decorative articles.

The most particularly ornamented fabrics and articles found in Rajasthan are often those for personal adornment. In Rajasthan, some form of embroidery invariably embellishes the three garments worn by women, the *kanchli, ghaghras* and *odhni*. Similarly men's garments like the *angarkha, achkan* and *jama* also display certain elements of embroidery. It is also used to beautify the household items, like bedspreads, wall hangings and animal trappings. Where embroidery is done for domestic use, it is by custom a feminine occupation. Rajasthani men, traditionally, were involved in embroideries like zardosi and danka. These crafts receive the patronage of royal families even today.

As in many traditional societies, Rajasthani women lead somewhat restricted lives. Embroidery, thus, becomes the expression of a woman's artistic temperament. These are often leisure time activities, after the daily chores are done. A wide variety of techniques are used in the embroidery of costumes and textiles. Some of the popular styles are, metal embroidery, gota work, and pichwai.

The different communities of Rajasthan have their own style of embroidery. In Bikaner and Jaisalmer the embroidered leather saddles are very popular. The Jaisalmer embroidery also applies mirror works sometimes to provide a visual impact. Embroidery practiced in Bikaner is done by counting threads. Women of Sikar and Jhunjhuna make animal figures and simple tree forms in their embroidery. In their work, all these remain juxtaposed together to form a specific pattern in the borders of their blue and black cotton skirts. The *odhanis* are also embroidered with animal figures and vegetable patterns. Women of Barmer use mirrors, thus enhancing the beauty of the embroidered piece.

These embroidery works of Rajasthan are part of its tradition. But now, it is widely used as an occupation and is highly praised by the tourists all over the world.

ZARDOZI EMBROIDERY

Zardozi or Zari or *kalabattu* is an embroidery work done in metal wires. Jaipur, Ajmer, Tonk and Jodhpur are important centres for zari work in Rajasthan. Zardozi involves the use of gold threads, spangles, beads, seed pearls, wire, gota and kinari. The art of this embroidery is mostly passed on from generation to generation. The fabric on which the work has to be done is first mounted on a wooden frame called *adda*, and the tracing of the design is done. Then the embroiderer starts embroidery. We can broadly categories the zari handwork in four categories- dapka, salma or nakshi, arri work and badla work.

Dapka: Dapka is a very detailed type of needle work. At least three to four workers are required for a detailed and fine work at the same time on the same piece. First a thick cotton cord is stitched on the pattern to be embroidered. Then on this cord prefabricated zari thread is looped on with an ordinary stitching needle. The patterns mostly made are of flowers, leaves, and peacock.

Salma or nakshi: Salma or nakshi is cheaper than dapka and is slightly less exquisite. A wedding skirt and mantle (lehanga and odhani) cannot be complete without nakshi as it shines much more than dapka. Nakshi puts life in the art work. The work commences from exterior to interior, that is, the outline of the motif is worked with the twisted metallic wire *gigai*, followed by filling with twisted circular metallic wire, the Salma. For fixing the accessories, back, running, chain, couching stitch is employed. Meenakari, the enamel effect, is also combined with Salma work.

The motifs comprised of floral and geometrical patterns and are popular with distinctive names like Ganga-jamuna (blend of gold and silver thread), jamavar (overall elaborate trellised pattern), Bel (trellised border), Hazar butas (fine work with glittering thousands butties), Katao ki bel (scalloped trellis border) and so on.

Arri work: Arri work is a more delicate form of embroidery. It is done with both coloured and golden thread. The thread is put on the tip of a arri needle which is passed through the cloth giving chain-stitch-like impressions.

Badla Work: In this work, metal ingots are melted and pressed through perforated steel sheets to convert into wires. They are then hammered to the required thinness. Plain wire is called badla, and when wound round a thread, it is called kasab. Smaller spangles are called sitara and tiny dots made of badla are called mukaish.

GOTA KINARI WORK

Gota work or Lappe ka kaam is a well known form of metal embroidery of Rajasthan, India. The embroiderers of Jaipur, Bikaner, Ajmer, Udaipur and Kota are famous for their unique styled gota work all over the world. On religious, social and festive occasions, men, women and children dress in their finest clothes that are often ornamented with Gota work or Lappe ka kaam. This style of embroidery was started by Mugals and spreaded to the courts of various states like Rajasthan.

This work is mostly done in remote villages of Jaipur, by local people called *"khandani karigars"*, as an inherited art. There is no better choice than 'Gota Work' when Rich & Heavy look is desired in Light weight. It is also low cost & durable.

Raw Material: The gota work is done on pure georgette, chiffon, velvet & silk. The colours commonly used were red, orange, pink, magenta, maroon & yellow. Gota is a band of gold or silver that is produced in different widths and woven in satin weave. Badla or a metal yarn that is made of beaten gold or silver forms the warp and silk or cotton is used in the weft. Depending on its width, Gota work or Lappe ka kaam can be found under different names like *chaumasiya* and athmasiya. Various types of gotta are *sikhiya gotta* (simple tape), *lappa gota* (twill woven tape), *siru gota* (striated tape), *thappa gota* (heat set tape), *gokhru* (hand crimpled tape), *chaumasa, panchmasa, athmasa, lehru gotta, nakshi, bijbel, bijiya, and kiran.*

In real Gota, silver & gold metals are used. But now-a-days the base metal is copper, coated by silver etc. Sometimes, copper has been replaced by polyester film which is metalized & coated as per requirements. This has resulted in better quality at lower cost.

Variety of gota work garments and textiles were used by the royalty, members of the court, temple idols and priests, as well as for altar cloths at shrines and prayer offerings.

Technique: The base fabric is tied on four sides with thick cords and is attached to a wooden frame known as *"Khaat"*. Design is traced with tracing paper by *safeda* or chalk powder spreading over it. According to the outlines of the design Gota is cut and folded into different shapes or it may be stitched in a simple line. Kinari or edging refers to the art of fringed border decoration.

Gota work or "Lappe ka kaam" is worked on fabric with the appliqué technique. With a slight hemming or simple running stitch, stylish designs flow from the artisan's fingers on to the garment. Some sections of the pattern are filled with coloured satin, thus resulting in a rich design that resembles the enameled jewellery of the region.

Now-a-days different shapes in different sizes are cut out of the Gota-Strip used in combination of other materials like *Dori, Sitara, Kundan* etc to create extraordinary effects.

Motifs: Trendy and attractive designs consisting of flowers, leaves, stylized mango motifs and heart shapes are usually worked on various kinds of *odhni* and *ghaghras*. Each pattern and motif had its own distinguishing name. Checkerboard patterns are also commonly used in gota work of Rajasthan. Animal figures, like parrot, peacock and elephant are some of the popular motifs. As a variation, floral designs are cut from gota and embroidered on to the cloth.

Products: The gota method is commonly used for women's formal costumes. Gota lacing is extremely popular and *odhni* and turban edges of Rajasthan are often worked with it. Many printed or embroidered *ghaghras* are also trimmed with gota work. Men and women of all communities wear garments of Gota work or "Lappe ka kaam", as it is auspicious and essential during ceremonial occasions. Traditional articles like *Kurti, kaanchli, Saree, Lehanga*, dress for idols, turbans, garments, baskets, thalposh or platter covers, and hookah are adorned with Gota work. Contemporary articles included *Kurtis, Salwar* and sarees, decorative panels and cushion covers are also in fashion.

RABARI EMBROIDERY

The Rabaris are a wandering community known for their extraordinary capacity for survival and adaptation in the arid regions of Gujarat and Rajasthan. They are recognized for their distinctive arts, especially embroidery, beadwork and mirrored mud sculpture. They also traditionally spin the wool from their sheep and give it to local weavers to make the woolen skirts, veils, blankets and turbans. Rabaris embroider a wide range of garments, bags, household decorations and animal trappings. Important events, rites and values in their lives are highlighted in the embroidery.

Unmarried girls traditionally embroider blouses, skirts, veils, wall hangings, pillows, purses and *Kothalo* which are dowry sacks. Married women embroider children's clothing and cradle cloth as well. They use little mirrors in their children's clothing, which are supposed to protect their children from evil spirits. Rabaris embroider camel trappings to honour the camels they still keep for ceremonial use. Rabari grooms wear elaborately embroidered long jackets and chorani pants, and brides wear ghaghara or skirts. Specific motifs and their composition have a name and meaning. Many of these symbols represent elements intrinsic to Rabari's everyday life and throws light upon how the community sees their world.

PATTU EMBROIDERY OF RAJASTHAN

Jaisalmar is very famous for all its craftsmanship. Woolen pattu of this place is unique in design and quality. These days the traditional designs have been made contemporary. Along with this, the famous embroidery mirror work is also very beautiful and adds to the beauty of pattu work. Pretty articles of pattu work are available from costumes, home furnishings, jackets, caps and commercial items.

JAISELMER APPLIQUE WORK

The traditional 'Ralli' quilts, made by patchwork, are famous of Jaisalmer. The quilt is made by sewing several layers of old fabrics, where the upper most layer being made of new cotton cloth. The colours used for patch work are olive green, brown, maroon and black. The corners are decorated with tassels of cotton or silk and sequins called *'Phuladi'*. *Cholies*, saddle cloth, bed spreads, cushion covers and purses are some of the products decorated by Jaisalmer Appliqué art.

SUJANI WORK

The sujani work of eastern Rajasthan is of a very fine quality and is inspired by the original suzani art of Bihar and Kantha of Bengal. An old cloth is folded three or four times and stitched together and new cloth is then attached over it. Embroidery is done using chain and running stitch. Creepers, flowers, and peacock design are common. This sujani style of embroidery is used for making winter wear, especially *sadaris* (jackets). In earlier times, this work was done on scabbards, shield-cushions, and on covers for gun-powder bags.

MOTI BHARAT

Moti bharat is an art of Jalor district of Rajasthan. This work is not done on the fabric. The opaque white beads form the base on which the transparent beads are worked by stringing them together in various shapes and forms. Traditionally blue, green yellow and red coloured beads are commonly used. Stylized human figures, geometrical designs, glimpses of daily life, horse and camel riders, elephant with *haudha*, horse with carriage, the famous love legend of local hero "Dhola" and his lover "Maru" are the designs repeatedly used. Various articles like, purse, cap, *toran*, play articles, cradle decoration and showpieces are prepared in Moti Bharat embroidery.

MEO EMBROIDERY

The Meos of Alwar has their unique style of embroidery. They embroider rich patterns with chain stitch in contrasting colours either white or black and the body is covered with the darning stitches as in phulkari, in golden yellow colour. Green, red and purple colour is sparsely used. The base material is handspun & hand woven Khaddar and thread employed is silk floss. Dancing figures, flowers and peacocks are the commonly used motifs. The embroidery is generally done on dresses like long skirts locally called *ghagras* and mantles or *odhanis* and on footwear, cloak draped over the oxen etc. Uniqueness of Meo embroidery lies in the balanced effect of geometrical forms with circular movements.

KNUCKLEPAD EMBROIDERY

There are several communities of Rajasthan, who are involved in making leather products and embroideries on them. In the 'knucklepad' leather products, miniature landscapes and festive scenes are embroidered like in Rajput paintings. The minute details of the embroidery are worked out and the group compositions are done carefully. The scenes embroidered here are mainly of human figures as well as floral and bird designs.

RELIGIOUS EMBROIDERIES OF RAJASTHAN

JAIN EMBROIDERY

Jain occupies the main trading population of Rajasthan. Rajasthan is home for various religious shrine and temples of Janis. During ceremonial occasions and festivals, it is customary to offer some gifts to these holy places and this is how the religious embroideries of Rajasthan have taken birth. The origin of the Jain embroidery goes back sixteenth century.

Material: The base material is satin in blue red or violet colour. Sometimes the rich looking soft velvet is also used as base material.

Stitches: Basic stitches comprised of stem, satin and chain stitch. Embroidery is worked with silk floss of blue, green, yellow and white colours, along with little combination of silver thread, to add to the luster.

Motifs: The basic concept of Jain Philosophy has been pictured on the articles made with the embroidery. Mandala is the main floral motif. The embroidery depicts Jain beliefs & shows different parts of heaven where various gods and goddesses live. Adivipa are representation of cosmology, which depicts universe and the *mangla* or *astha mangalika* implies at suspicious projects, related to eight Jain *Tirthankers*. There was great influence of court embroideries during eighteenth and nineteenth century which is evident on some of the article where human figures have been dressed similar to court people.

PICHWAI EMBROIDERY

In the temples of Rajasthan, a cloth hanging named 'Pichwai of Nathdwara' can be found, which is very nicely embroidered. Pichwais are generally used as a decoration in temples. Pichwais are traditionally painted textiles but these are also available in printed and embroidered form.

Material: The traditional pichwai is made on coloured cotton, satin or velvet fabric. The fabric choice varies with season; summer and winter.

Colours: Generally, the pichwai has red cotton background and the embroidery is done in cream, green, yellow and black. White colour is used for the outlines. In some cases, the embroidery is done with golden and silver threads to highlight the design. In few case Pichwai are also made of applique work, where the basic material is invariably red in colour.

Motifs: The traditional Pichwai has "Shree nath ji" with his dark blue face, under ever green tree surrounded by his play mates and cows. The motifs are wide variety picked up from nature. Animal motifs like cows, calves and fish, bird motifs like parrot and peacock are embroidered in pichwai. Kalka and lotus flowers are also found. In pichwai, mythological motifs like Ganesh, Hanuman and Surya are also used.

The pilgrims get Pichwai ordered where the devotee himself gives out line of the design and the actual embroidery is done by mochi, gold and silver workers.

TRADITIONAL RAJASTHANI MOTIFS

Gota Work Motif

Gota Kinari Work

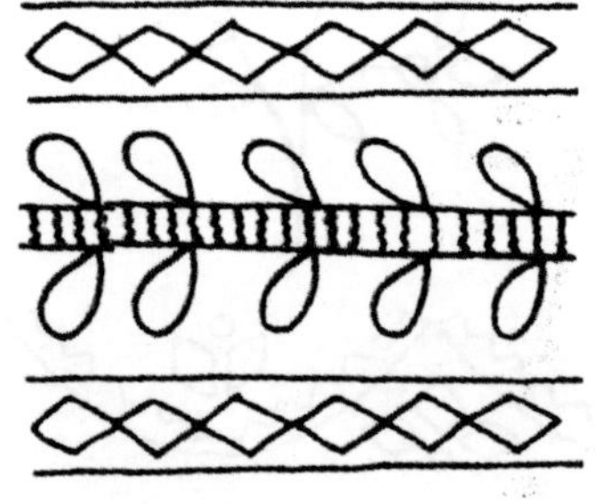

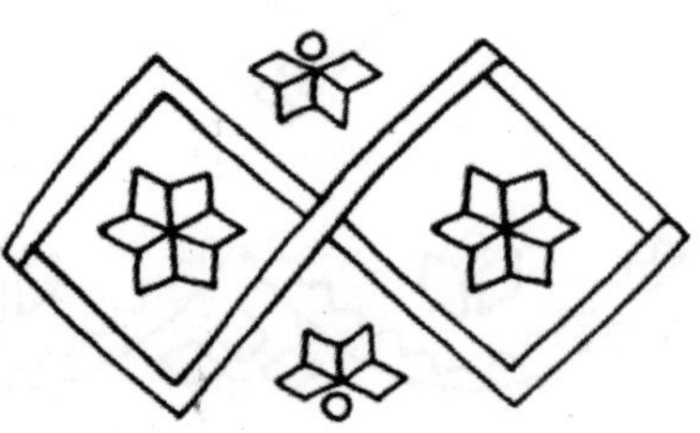

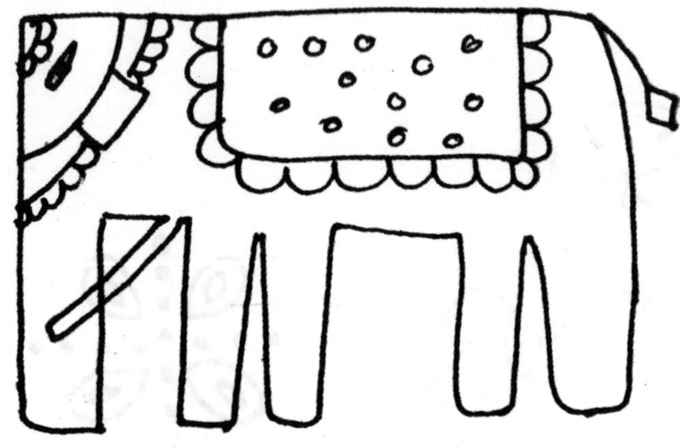

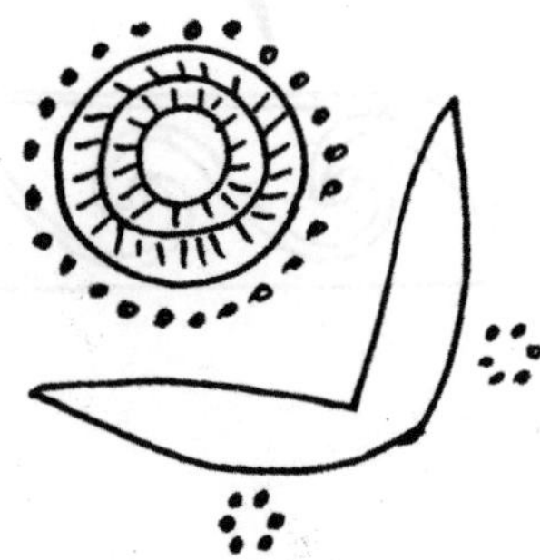

CHAPTER 8

Kantha Embroidery of West Bengal

India has a rich heritage of the art, music, dance, sculpture, architecture, metalwork, embroidery and so on. Among them Indian embroideries expresses unity in diversity because the art of embroidery exhibited by Indians who lived widely region wise. The embroidery folk art of Bengal is famous as "Kantha". It is also called as the "Recycling Art". 'Kantha' is a Sanskrit word, which means `Rags`. Kantha work refers to the application of simple running stitch covering the entire surface. Kanthas were produced in Hugli, Patna, and Satagaon, Faridpur, Khulna & other parts of East & West Bengal. This embroidery gives a typical example of how a simple stitch can create elaborate motifs.

Traditionally, this type of embroidery was an art practiced by Bengali women in their spare time and has limitless opportunities for this type of designs innovations. This embroidery is a very good example of simple, creative, and economic way to make something useful and beautiful by using old sarees. It is also said that a true Kantha narrates a story and portrays the emotions and the life of the artist.

Story of Kantha Embroidery

There are several legends that are associated with the origin of this art form. It is said that in the past, the precious clothes that were torn out were piled in layers and stitched by the women of West Bengal. Another legend relates Kantha origin to lord Buddha and his disciples because they used the thrown away rags to cover themselves. They used to stitch those thrown away rags.

The oldest extant Kantha date from the early 1800s and is embroidered with blue, black and red threads that were unraveled from saree borders. Because they were salvaged from used garments that had been frequently laundered, the colours tend to be muted.

Fabric: Fabrics used for Kantha were old fabrics. Old saree or *dhoti's* pieces were neatly joined together in layers in running stitch using white thread drawn from the fabric itself. The edges were tucked together. The female of Bengal mostly wore white saree hence the base material was always white for Kanthas.

Threads: The threads used for embroidery were usually drawn from the colourful borders of the discarded sarees.

Colour: The white cotton thread is used for joining purpose and for embroidery. The colourful threads of blue, red, yellow, green and black are also used for forming the figure.

Stitches: The joy of the Kantha is in the simplicity of the design and the stitch. The fabric is covered in running stitches which change colour and direction to form design. It is the way in which quite extraordinary results can be achieved using running stitch only.

Stitches used in Kantha embroidery are running, darning, tiny satin stitch. Stem stitch is also used to outline the figures. Running stitch or darning stitch is the main stitch used in Kantha. It is done in two ways- one in which stitches are formed randomly and other in which stitches are aligned in different rows. The great length of stitch is broken into tiny tacking which give almost a dotted appearance on either side of the cloth.

The size & thickness of Kantha varied according to its type. The layers of pieces are sewn together by simple darning stitch in white thread. The design motifs are first outlined with thread followed by focal points and then the filled with the colourful running stitch. *Kantha* gives a slight wrinkled, wavy effect to the surface on which it is done which is a typical feature associated with this embroidery. The basic stitch used is running stitch, though a wide variation of this simple stitch is also applied and these are: basic running stitch done in random way, running stitch in form of Jal, mat formation, even running stitch, diagonal arrangement (tercha), "V" shaped filling, spiral and circular filling and interlacing.

Motifs: The work of the Hindu and Muslim women differs in the kind of motifs and the patterns used. The Muslim women use more geometrical patterns and floral motifs, while the kantha made by Hindu women were pictorial and narrative, with forms from daily life, composed around a central floral motif. The design usually relies on a central circular form occupied by a many petalled lotus flower and four mango or tree motifs to mark the four directional axis. The space between the lotus and the trees is filled in with figures, objects and symbolic motifs.

- **Floral motifs:** Creepers, floral, scrolls and spirals, trees, *kalka*, *mandala*, foliage, tree of life, *satadala padma* or lotus (usually in the center)
- **Animal motif:** Dancing peacock, swan, lion, birds, fish, elephant, eagle, deer running, snake
- **Other motifs:** Boat, submarine sceneries, ships, pitcher, mermaid, mirror, nut cracker, umbrella, chariot, palanquine, temples, *hukka*, sun, wheel and *swastik* etc.

Sometimes themes are also taken from the day to day lives. Motifs are also taken from well-known epics such as the Ramayana or Krishna-lila, and also legends evolving from folk-rituals of Bengal. The field is filled with the patterns like tree, animal figures, birds, fishes, boats, chariots and mythological stories. The border consists of creepers, floral, scrolls and spirals.

The lotus motif is the most common motif found in kanthas. This motif is associated with Hindu iconography and thus is also very popular in the kantha. The lotus is the divine seat. There are various forms of lotus motifs, from the eight-petal *astadal padma* to the hundred petal *satadal*. In the older Kanthas, the central motif is almost always a fully bloomed lotus. The solar motif is closely associated with the lotus motif, often found together in the centre. The solar motif symbolizes the life giving power of the sun. Wheel is also very popular motif in Kantha.

Different Types of Kanthas

Indian Kantha is a fine example of rich tradition of handicrafts still blossoming in rural India. There are different types of Kantha, named according to its utility.

1. **Lep (Shawl):** this is a thick quilt wrap used in the winters as covers. The designs of lep were geometrical with running stitch. These are intricately embroidered shawls of woolen, cotton and silk. While making shawls, the cloth is given layers that are kept together by the stitches. These shawls were earlier made in Bengal to protect people from severe cold.
2. **Sarfani:** this is also a wrap or cover and used for ceremonial purpose
3. **Bayton:** it is used as a wrap for book and valuable goods. It is square in shape. It has a central motif and 2-3 borders. Border may have human and animal figures. A lotus or *satadala padma* is in the center. The four corners being covered with trees, flowers and leaves. This Kantha was meant to be carring during journeys and to be presented to the relatives.

4. **Orr:** it is rectangular in shape used as a pillow case. The designs are trees and birds, creeper and foliage with border.
5. **Arsilata:** it is used as a wrap for mirrors and combs. It has a wide border with lotus in center. Creepers, trees and spirals are other motifs.
6. **Durjani:** this is also known as '*thalia*'. It is square in shape and is supposed to be the wallet covers. Kantha has an embroided border with lotus in center.
7. **Rumal:** this is handkerchief. Center motif is lotus around which variety of motifs are arranged.
8. **Sujni:** generally large and rectangular in shape. It is a bed spread, the most intricate kantha entirely covered with gods, animals, birds, fish and floral motifs. It has 2-3 borders for strengthening them to prevent tearing. The lotus being the central motif, scenes from Ramayana and folk tales are embroidered into the space between trees and lotus.

Contemporary Kantha: Today, Kantha embroidery work has become the fashion label in the Indo-Western world. The contemporary Kantha is not necessarily done on old multiple layered sarees or dhotis. It can also be seen on the present day garments like the sarees, *dupatta,* shirts for men and women, bedding and other furnishing fabrics. For these articles and dresses the base fabric used is cotton and silk. These days, new fabric is used instead of old.

TRADITIONAL KANTHA MOTIFS

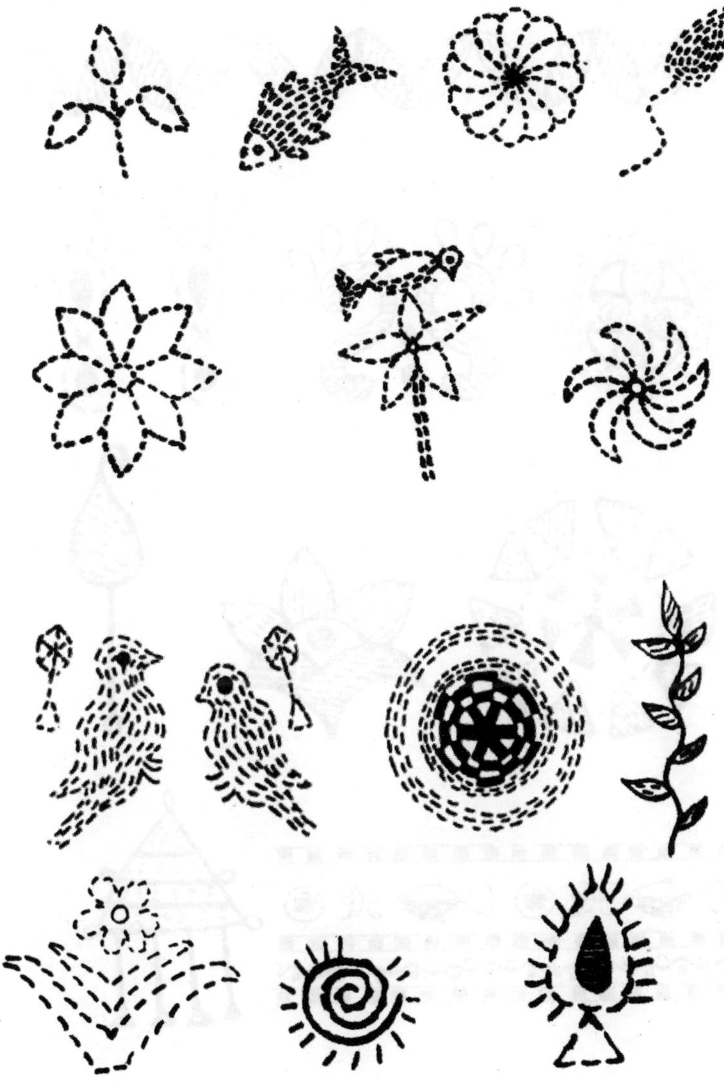

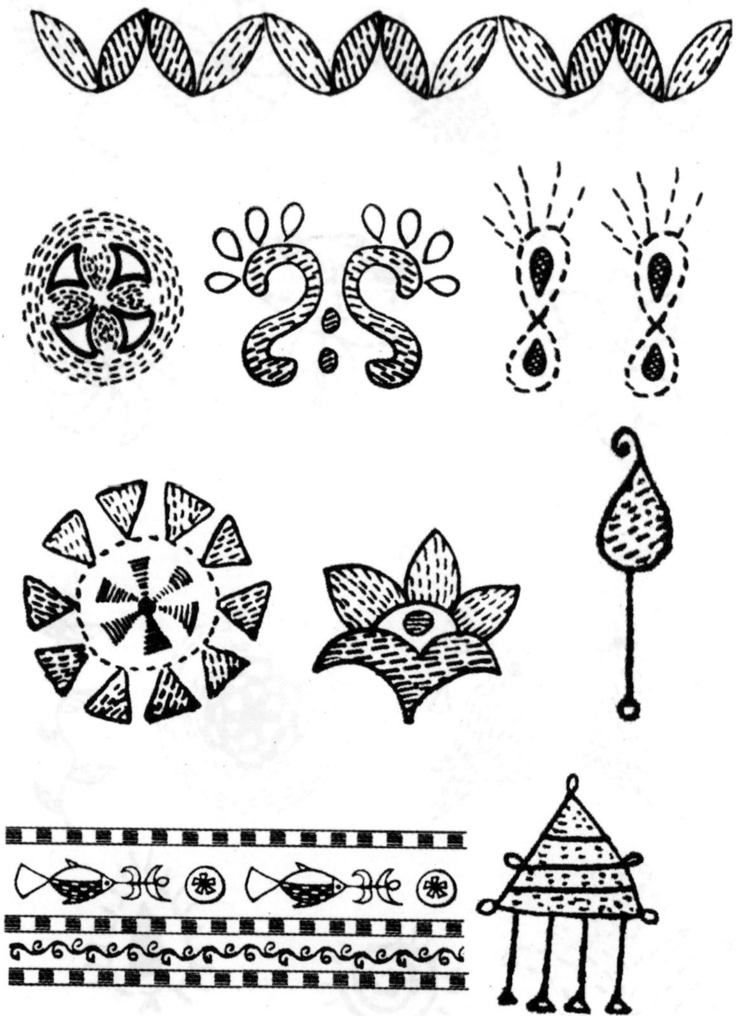

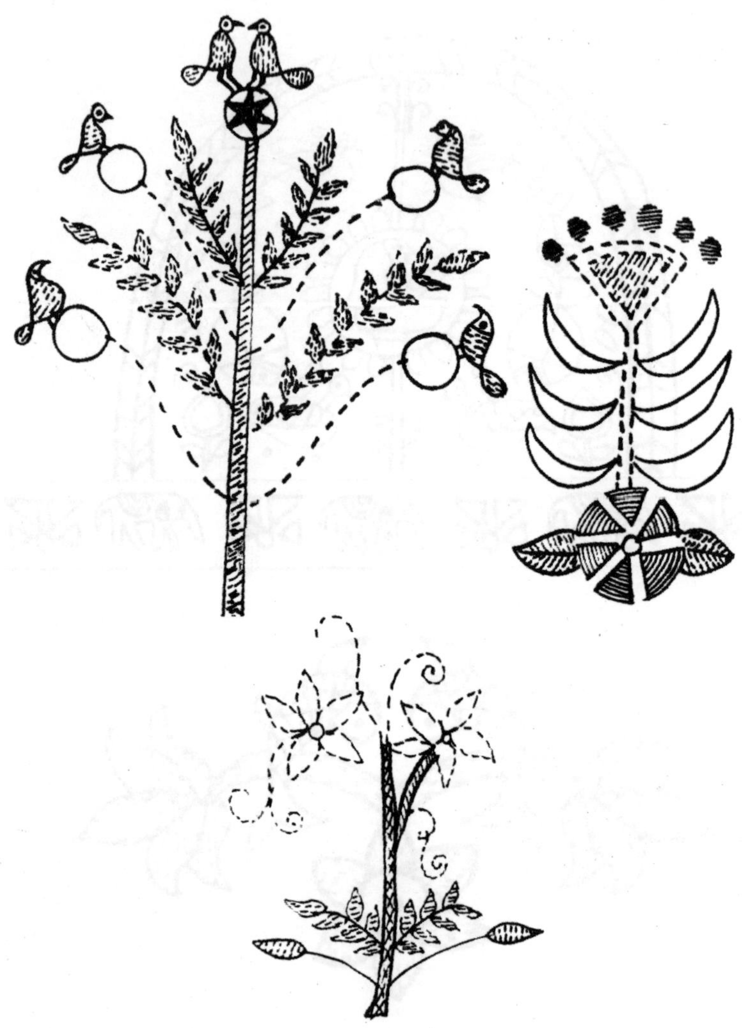

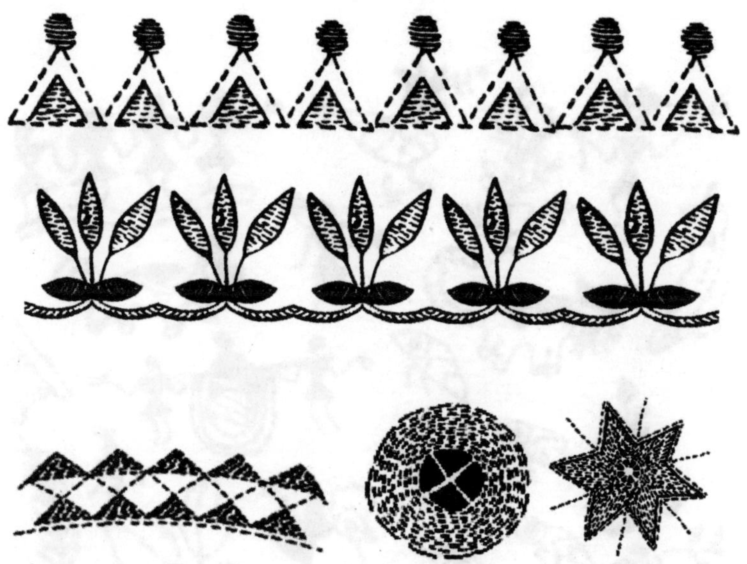

CHAPTER 9
Embroideries of Bihar

INTRODUCTION

Embroidery has a unique place in the history and civilization of a country. Bihar is also famous for its simple and very beautiful embroidery techniques, like other states of India. Kashida, Khatwa, Suzni Kantha and mirror work are famous embroidery forms of Bihar.

SUJNI KANTHA OF BIHAR

Sujni is a unique embroidery art of Bihar reflects the charm and simplicity. The Sujni of Bihar is very similar to the Kantha of Bengal and is also a woman's tradition. Embroidery in Bihar is passed from mother to her daughter as a craft. Sujni is practiced in different part of Bihar like Patna, Madhubani and Muzaffarpur.

Story of Sujni Embroidery

Sujni kantha craft was originally practised only by Rajput women of Bihar. Initially sujni was made for traditional purposes– to wrap the newborn. Sujni was meant to wrap a newborn in a soft embrace, resembling that of a mother. New cloth was considered to be harsh on its skin, thus old clothes were used. The term sujani perfectly reflects the above-mentioned function– *"su"* means easy and facilitating, while *"jani"* means birth.

In sujni work patches of different coloured cloth from old sarees were sewn together. These pieces were then quilted and embroidered in deferent designs to make small quilts called sujni for newly-born babies.

Fabric: Sujni embroidery is done on fine muslin fabric. The base fabric is generally red or white. It is made by old materials like sarees or dhotis. Sarees or dhotis in this area are predominantly white and border in black or red or blue.

Stitch: Sujni embroidery is very simple but requires a lot of patience and time. The motifs are filled with running stitches with short gaps. The outlines of the main motifs are highlighted with thick chain stitch.

Colour: The inner spaces of the motifs are filled with threads of vibrant colours. Chain stitch usually in black, brown and red thread is done for the main outline of the motif.

Motifs: The design of these products interprets a mother's emotion and imagination regarding her baby. Design is mainly the depiction of mother's dream for her new born. The sujini depicts scenes such as bride in palanquin, dancing peacocks, boy hurried kite, etc. Beautiful embroidery of gods and goddesses was also done and hung on walls. The artisans also create floral, animal and bird motifs on both cotton and silk that have immense popularity in the local market.

A very common motif includes a deity, Chitiriya Ma, the Lady of the Tatters. Other fertility oriented motifs and patterns include the sun and moon (life giving forces), animal and bird motifs and fantastic winged animals for protection against destructive forces, and motifs to attract the blessings of their gods.

The outline of design is traced or drawn directly on to the cloth by the women. Stories, compositions and colour combination are worked out by the women on their own.

Contemporary sujni articles: In Sujni embroidery artisans make bed sheets, sarees, *dupattas*, dress materials, cushion cover, wall hanging, shirt and bags. Sujni products are used for decorative as well as utilitarian purposes. For making these articles, casement fabric is sometimes used. Coloured mulmul or handloom is used for sarees, *kurtas,* and *dupattas.* Tussar silk is predominantly used for creating attractive garments and sarees.

KHATWA APPLIQUE

The applique work of Bihar is called "Khatwa". People in some villages of Bihar are involved only in art works and it is their main source of income. The khatwa appliqué of Bihar has the same origin as sujuni- the desire to make the best out of waste. The production centers of this craft are Patna city, Muzaffarpur and Madhubani district. It consists of applique work on cloth with chain and straight stitch embroidery. The traditional khatwa had reverse applique in which a layer a cloth is applied onto a base cloth. The top layer has incisions or slashes that are folded and stitched down, revealing the pattern with the colour of the base cloth. Cut motifs are stitched on the base material according to an abstract or narrative design. Traditional motifs are drawn from nature and their day to day life like man, bird, leaves, beehives, bee, plants, flowers, creepers and animals like elephant.

Khatwa is mainly used to create designer tents, canopies, *shamianas* and much more. Making of such tents involves work by both men and women. While cutting of clothes is done by men, women use their expertise in stitching part. Khatwa is also used in designing women garments. A thick fabric and geometric patterns are used while making the tents on important occasion or functions. The contemporary products made are *sarees, dupattas,* cushion covers, bed and sofa covers, curtains, table cloths and wall hangings.

KASHEEDA OF BIHAR

Kasida of Bihar is widely practiced by women al over the Bihar for personal use. Articles of daily use like blouses, baby's cap, kamarband (sash), takias (pillow covers), border of sarees or odnis are normally embroidered. The embroidery has three different types of stitches leads to the development of distint style.

1. **Jhinkana Embroidery:** Jhinkana is chain stitch, used to beautify the items of personal clothing. Chain stitch is done on personal garments and most commonly on blouses. The patterns they make are jewellary patterns like sat-larda-haar (seven stringed necklace), and necklace with pandent. Peacock or elephant with rider is also commonly embroidered on blouses. The needle makes a light sound when working its way through the cloth, thus called "Jhinkana". Exclusive designs are created by women with this embroidery.
2. **Bharat Work:** bharat work is generally done over the entire surface. This is somewhat similar to the bagh of Punjab. The embroidery here follows the warp and weft of woven fabric. The designs are generally ractangles, squares, wavy lines, diamond and simple flower motifs. The embroidery is generally done on red cloth with white thread with the effective use of yellow and bottle green.
3. The third variety is a combination of chain stitch done with appliqué of cloth. it is practiced on cap and blouses.

MIRROR WORK OF BIHAR

The Mithila region of Bihar is the centre for embroidery with mirror work. The women folk of this area create garments specially children's garments and items that suit the purpose of home decor. Red, blue, and black, on bleached hand-woven cloth is used for the purpose. The designs are usually folk or religious motifs along with stripes, lines and animal motifs. Mirror work is done on many fabrics and these mirrors are supported with the chain stitch using the cotton, silk and synthetic threads.

Apart from these embroidery works, the artisans of Bihar are well known for creating designs with Zari work. The artisans also create geometrical patterns that resemble the kasuti embroidery of Mysore and have wide range of variations and styles. This is done in both silver and gold metallic threads to make the motifs of birds, leaf etc.

EMBROIDERY MOTIFS OF BIHAR

Khatwa Design

A Suzni Cover

Applique Work with Bird Motif

Applique Work

CHAPTER 10

Kasuti Embroidery of Karnataka

Kasuti embroidery is the world famous and typical traditional form of art mainly practiced in Karnataka. The word "kasuti" can be broken into two parts- "kai", means hand and "suti", means cotton, and hence signifies the hand work on cotton. The word "Kasuti" also means embroidery in the Kannada language, its Marathi equivalent being Kashida, so it is also called as Kashida of Karnataka. This embroidery is mainly performed in Dharwar, Bijapur, Belgaum, Miraj, Sangli, Hubli and Jamakhandi districts of Karnataka. The most remarkable feature of kasuti is that it is identical on both sides when done skillfully. It is a domestic art that has now taken on commercial forms. The embroidery is very simple and can cover large areas in a short period of time. Kasuti work is quite popular on Ilkal silk sarees of Karnatka. These sarees are woven on pit loom with cotton material.

STORY OF KASUTI

The origin of Kasuti embroidery can be traced back to the period of *Chalukyas* when a great renaissance in the sphere of art and architecture took place. They encouraged cults of lord *Shiva* and built temples all over the south; the prominent among those are the cave temples of *Badami*, temples of Madurai, Thanjore and Kanchipuram. The women who witnessed these building operations gave expression to their artistic urge through some colourful artwork such as Kasuti.

Kasuti embroidery is believed to have originated from north Karnataka which after that spreaded all over the region. Kasuti developed mostly in Lingayat community. A Lingayat bride wears a kasuti embroidered Ilkal saree woven with typical borders and colour combinations in dark red, green and black. The hand woven blouse with kasuti embroidery was considered the most appropriate gift for an expectant mother.

It is practiced mostly by women. Women of Karnataka expressed their artistic urge by embroidering delicate piece of colourful art, the kasuti. This art was passed from person to person and generation to generation. During leisure time the grandmothers used to teach kasuti to their grandchildren, daughter -in-law and neighbors. In olden days it was a custom that the bride had to possess a black silk saree called '*chandrakali* saree' with Kasuti work on it. Every woman was expected to adorn her saree and blouse with kasuti embroidery.

Fabric: It is done mostly on hand woven cotton cloth. Some families work this embroidery on matty cloth.

Threads: Silk thread was used in olden days. Now instead of silk yarns, mercerized cotton threads are also used. Two to four strands are used for fine and coarse work respectively. This may vary according to the type of material, motif and stitch employed.

Colours: The colours used for kasuti work are bright and clean- Red, orange, crimson, purple, green, green-yellow and blue. White is predominant on black background. Bright and contrast colour combinations are used to make design bold and clear. Black background cloth was used for children wear and sarees.

Motif: Hindu motifs are predominant in Kasuti. The motifs used in kasuti are taken from architecture (mainly temples), mythological stories and also from beautiful flora and fauna. Motifs are also inspired from religious symbols and objects that the women come across in their daily life. It is believed that earlier it was done only in geometrical motifs. The designs of kasuti were definite; they have their definite size and were produces with counting of threads.

- **Temple motifs:** *Gopuram* (temple tops)
- **Animal and birds motifs:** Elephant, peacock, sparrow, serpent, tiger, swan, pegion, deer
- **Floral motifs:** Various types of creepers, foliages, flowers, *Tulsi katte*, lotus border
- **Mythological motifs:** *Hanuman, rath* (chariot), *shankh, shivlinga, nandi* or sacred bull, palanquine, *swastika*
- **Other motifs:** lampshade, cradle, human figure, *aasana*, pedestal.

The larger designs feature like elephant, the temple, the basil (*Tulsi*) plant platform, Nandi the sacred bull etc were embroidered near the *pallu*. As they go down the length, the designs get smaller like flowers, birds, animals and variety of geometrical designs.

Stitches: stitches in kasuti are always vertical, horizontal and diagonal. The undisclosed fact of this age old embroidery form is that it can be done only by counting the threads of the warp and weft. Design is rare traced on the fabric to be embroidered. Two-six threads are used together to embroidery a unit on the fabric, depending upon the fineness of the design. Embroidery is started with a back stitch without knotting in the thread. The stitches used in this embroidery include

1. **Gavanti:** It has been derived from a Kannada word "*ganoti* or *gantu*" that means 'knot'. It is the most common and very simple stitch used in kasuti and really beautiful designs are formed with it alone. It contains back stitch or double running stitch in which the first running stitch is filled by the second running stitch on the same line.

This stitch looks similar in both sides. This may be used in vertical, horizontal or diagonal directions.

2. **Murgi**: It contains zigzag running stitch that gives the effect of ladder. It is same as gavanthi stitch but works in stepwise manner. The design in murgi stitch look similar on both sides of the fabric. Small motifs like square, triangle, ladder, flowers, hexagonal are made with this stitch. These small motifs are arranged further to form an elaborate geometric design.
3. **Menthi***:* Its name is derived from fenugreek (*methi*) seeds, in Karnataka. This is ordinary cross stitch that gives rich effect to the fabric. This cross stitch usually appears heavy as it is used for filling purpose. It is most commonly used to quickly cover up the background areas of design. This stitch requires more length of thread than the other three stitches and does not give same appearance on either sides of the cloth. It is mainly used in architectural patterns.
4. **Negi:** the literal meaning of negi in Kannada is 'to weave' i.e. negi design has an overall effect of a woven design. It involves ordinary running or darning stitches. It is mainly used for larger design. It is worked in long and short floats on fabric; therefore, design is not similar on both sides of fabric.

Kasuti Products: Traditionally it is done on garments like – Ilkal sarees, blouse (Bodice or choli), *Kulai* or *kunchi* (infant caps), *Lehnga* (skirt mainly for children) and other traditional garments. Now-a-days kasuti embroidery is also done on household linen like handkerchief, bed cover, sofa and cushion covers, curtains and garments like ladies suits and stoles.

KASUTI OF KARNATAKA

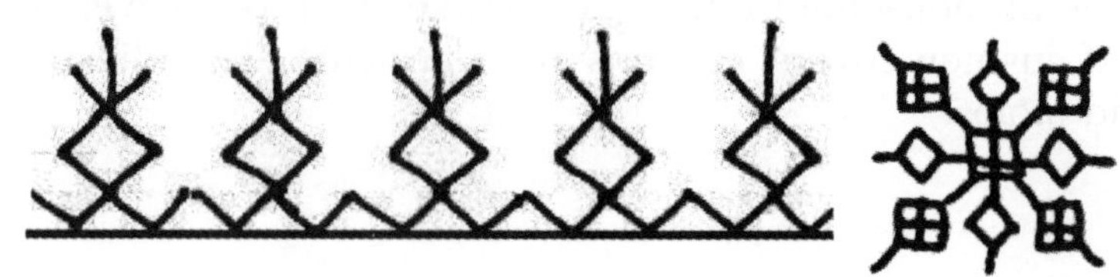

Motif in Murgi Stitch

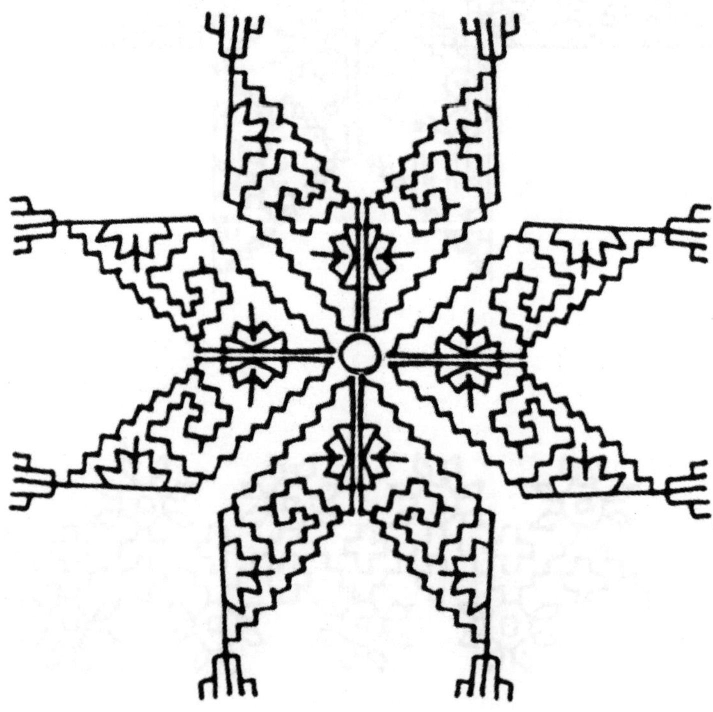

Motif in Murgi Stitch

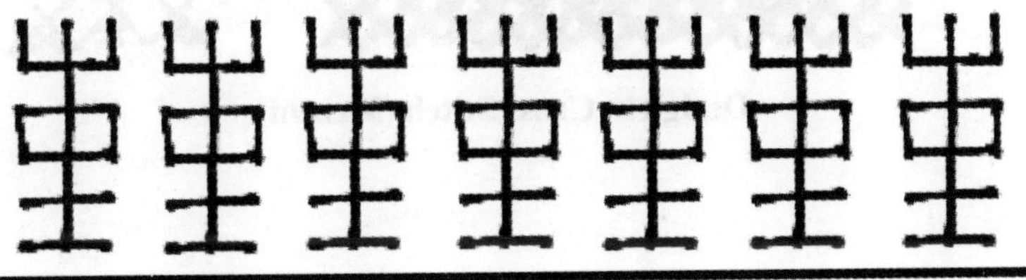

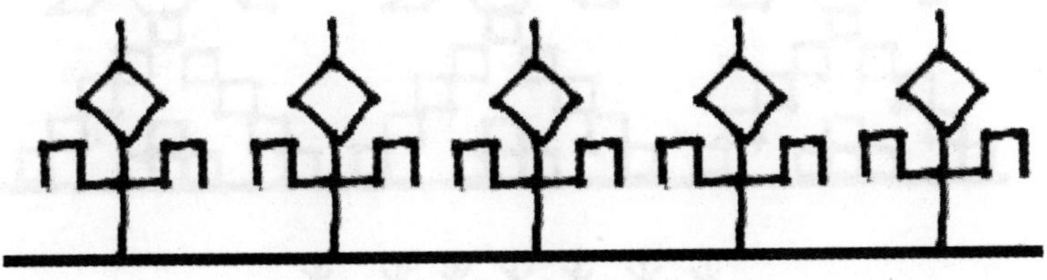

Design in Cross Stitch (Menthi)

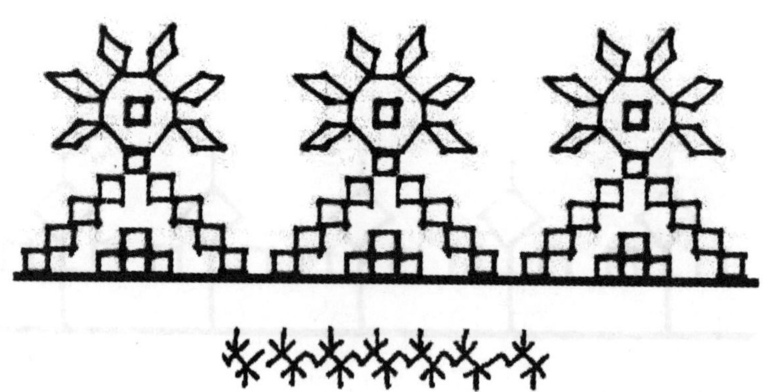

Motif in Menthi Stitch

Design in Gavanti Stitch

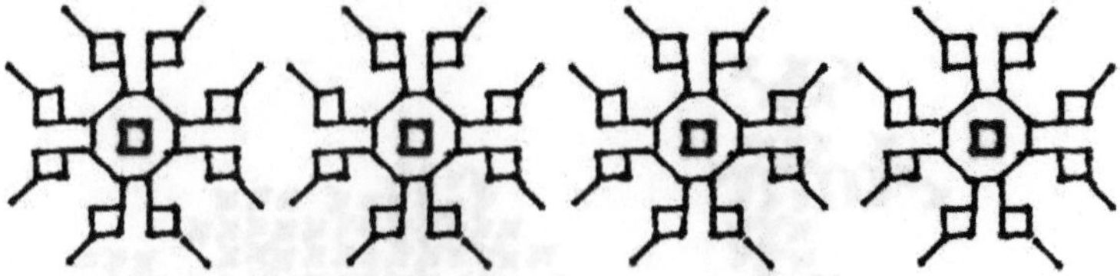

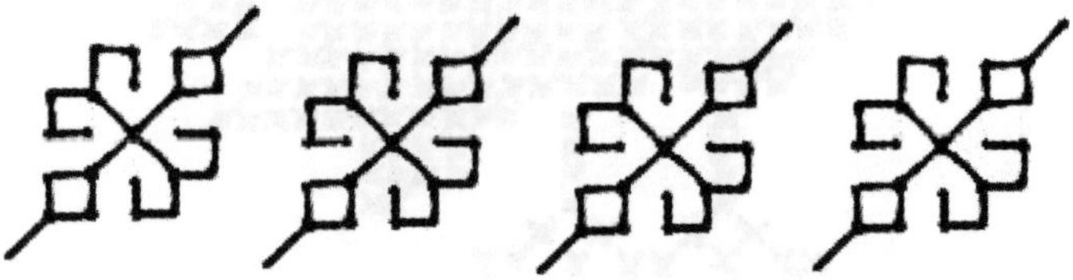

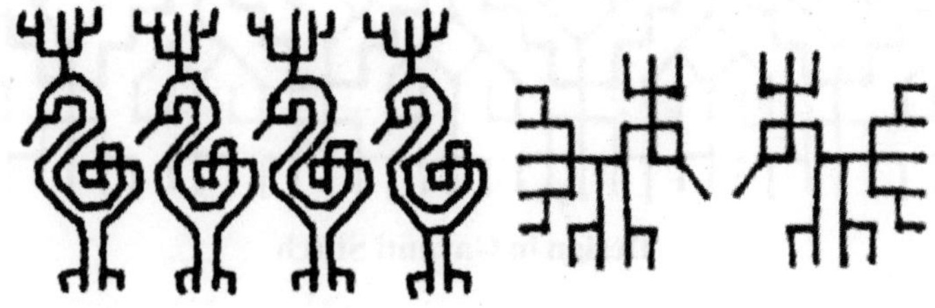

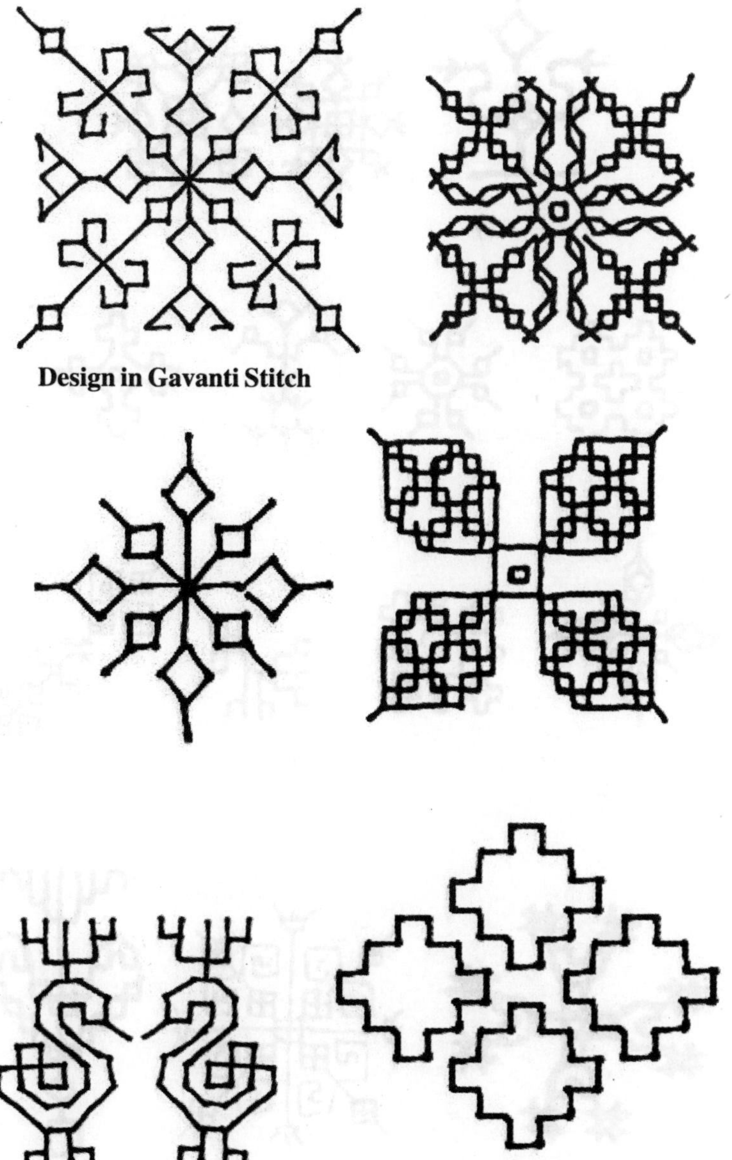

Design in Gavanti Stitch

Design in Negi Stitch

Palki Motif

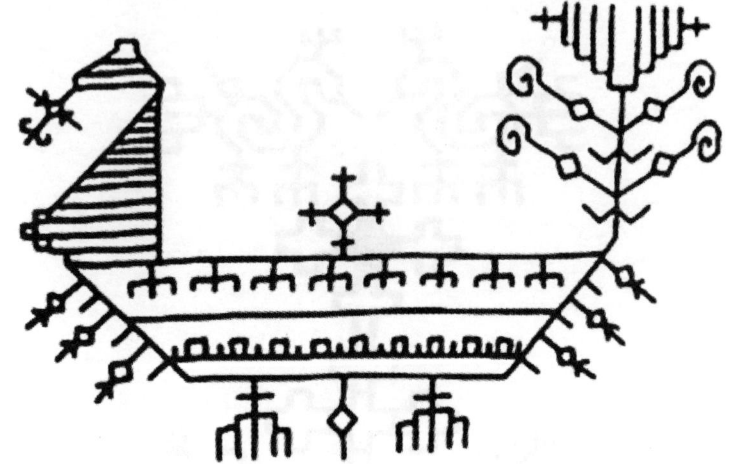

Peacock Motif

Deer Motif

CHAPTER 11
Embroidery of Manipur

India is known for its diverse culture that exist in harmony. Each culture and region has its own unique form of art and embroidery. The embroidery of each place has its roots in the culture of the region. Manipur is a beautiful state in northern India, surrounded by hills, valleys and lakes. The people of Manipur are skilled in many unique arts and crafts. The women of Manipur also do fine and delicate embroidery.

Story of Embroidery

The embroidery is usually done on the border of the *phaneyk* which is worn by women like a sarong. The *phaneyk* is a woven piece of fabric in dark stripes against a light background. It is woven by the women themselves. It is common to find a pit loom in almost every household in Manipur.

There are a number of other fabrics embroidered besides the *phaneyk*. These are specially made for warriors and to be presented by the king as a mark of distinction.

- **Zamphie:** It is a war cloth that is a special type of shawl embroidered by the women at home and is used by the warriors at the time of going out for war.

- **Ningthouphee:** It is a waistcoat, which is presented by the king to the warriors of the country.
- **Saijounba:** It is a long coat that is prepared with special embroideries for the very trusted courtiers of the king.
- **Phiran amba:** These are the small flags delicately embroidered and used by the warriors as plumes on their turbans, each designated the rank.
- **Namthang-khut-hut:** A design derived out of the head of *Pakhangba* on the wrapper, meant to be used only by the ladies of the royal family.
- **Khamenchatpa:** These designs are embroidered on the dhotis and are presented to the people of distinction.
- **Phiranji:** It is a red coloured blanket presented to the persons of merit. The colour of the blanket is totally red and is believed to have been copied from the blood with the placenta.

Fabric: Manipuri embroidery is done on woven cotton fabric. The fabric has normally black background colour to put emphasis on colours of the embroidery. Green and yellow is also used.

Threads and colours: Earlier untwisted silk threads were used for embroidery work. Now cotton threads are also used instead of silk. The colours used are shades of red, yellow, white, green, and black.

Stitches: Embroidery is mainly done with tiny satin chain and stem stitch. Chain stitch is mostly utilized for outlining the motifs. Romanian stitch is also used. The stitches are very fine and even that look like a part of weave.

Traditional Designs in Manipuri Embroidery

Akyobi design: A very interesting and common pattern used in Manipuri embroidery is Akyobi design, seen on the border of the phanek. The embroidery is done over the plain border of phanek using a dark thread. It is a circular design, one circle joining the other, with each circle being further broken up into patterns, each with a significant motif and special name. It is worked in two shades of red with a bit of black and white. This embroidery of Manipur is done in an elegant snake- like pattern. This particular design is said to be derived from the legendary snake, *pakhamba,* which was killed by the husband of a goddess. Some other believes that the central round motif (like a dot) is symbol of a bee which flies around the lotus flower sucking its honey. The four petals on the side of the dot are known as the 'moil' the tender most part of the lotus bud.

Hijai mayek: Hijai mayek- a boat design is another pattern embroidered in black and white, and is worn by widows, elderly women and at funerals. It shows running lines and circular movements. Other motifs used are battle scenes, swords etc. The stitches used are tiny satin stitch.

Khoi mayek: The half open circular designs are known as the khoi mayek which means a fishing hook.

The other motifs used are butterfly, elephant, cockerel etc,. The excellent embroidery work of Manipur display Angami Naga shawls that are embellished with animal motifs in black. Previously, this shawl was termed as 'sami lami phee' which means warrior cloth of wild animals. The artisans use bright colours like bright green, red, yellow, and white to create designs on the shawls. Apart from creating different items using different designs, the local inhabitants of Manipur has mastered *abhala* or mirror-embroidery work which they use for creating costumes for rasa dance.

The Meithei community of Manipur is excelled in the *tindogbi* design which has received inspiration from a silk caterpillar sitting on a castor leaf and eating it.

MANIPURI EMBROIDERY MOTIFS

Akyobi Design

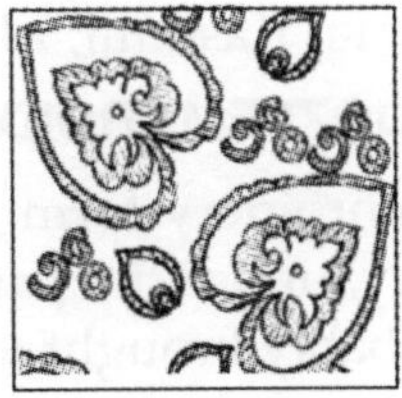

CHAPTER 12

Zardozi Embroidery

India has long been known for its embroidery done with gold and silver threads called Zardozi. Zari is gold, and zardozi embroidery is the glitteringly ornate, heavily encrusted gold thread work. The original embroidery of zari was done with pure silver wires coated with real gold known as *kalabatun*. Zardozi embroidery is beautiful metal embroidery, which once used to embellish the attire of the Kings and the royals in India. The traditional art of zari craft is practiced in many parts of India. Zardosi embroidery work is mainly a specialty of Lucknow, Agra, Bareilly, Varanasi, Delhi, Bhopal, Hyderabad, Kolkata, Kashmir, Mumbai, Ajmer and Chennai.

STORY OF ZARDOZI EMBROIDERY

A Persian embroidery form zardozi attained its summit in the 17th century, under the patronage of Mughal Emperor Akbar. It was probably brought to India by the Mughals. The word 'Zardozi' is made up of two Persian terms, "zar" meaning gold and "dozi" meaning embroidery. Zardozi adorned the costumes of the court, wall hanging, regal side walls of tents and the rich trappings of elephants and horses. Intricate patterns traced in gold and silver, studded with seed pearls and precious stones enhanced the shimmering beauty of silk, velvet and brocade. During Aurangzeb`s region, royal patronage to artists and craftsmen ceased and the royal ateliers were shutdown. Consequently, many craftsmen migrated to the neighbouring kingdoms of Rajasthan, Punjab and Gujarat to look for new patrons.

It can be envisaged that zardosi embroidery has been in existence in India from the time of the Rig Veda. There are numerous instances mentioning the use of zari embroidery as ornamentation on the attire of gods.

Types of Zardozi: Zari embroidery is done using gold and silver wires, with a crochet hook. The embroidery done gives the appearance of chain stitch. Zardozi, a more elaborate version of zari, involves the use of gold threads, spangles, beads, seed pearls, wire, gota and kinari.

Zardozi technique is mainly of two types:

1. **Karchobe style:** Generally done on velvet or heavy satin fabric with lining support, which is suitable for furnishing artifact and accessories.
2. **Kamdani style:** It is done on finer fabrics, suitable for costumes and related accessories such as muslin, silk etc.

Karchobe is further divided into five types:

1. **Kasab-Tiki:** Using gold and silver thread and spangles (tiki).
2. **Jhik-Tiki:** Using twisted thread and spangles.
3. **Chalak-Tiki:** Use of zigzag metal thread and spangles.
4. **Jhik-Chalak:** Using twisted metal thread called *jhik* and zig-zag thread called *chalak*.
5. **Bharat-Karachi:** Using pieces of cardboard to provide a raised body for the design, the material being used as padding.

Threads and material for zardozi work: Zardozi embroidery work involves making elaborate designs, using gold and silver threads. The *kalabatun* (gold or silver zari thread) thread is used for the work. Further adding to the magnificence of the work are the studded pearls and precious stones. The material used for zardozi work includes:

- **Tirora:** It is a gold thread spirally twisted, used in curves and complex designs.
- The dull zari thread is *'kora'* and lustrous one is *'chikna'*.
- **Sitara:** It is a small round metal piece to look like a star.
- **Gizai:** It is a circular thin stiff wire resembling an insect of this name.
- **Tilla:** it is a flat metal wire.
- **Salma:** these are stiff gold wires twisted like springs and cut to the required length before use.
- **Badla:** A flattened strip of metal wire is called badla.
- **Kasab:** badla when wound round on a silk or cotton thread, it is called kasab. Silver or gold-plated silver thread is also known as kasab.
- **Dabka:** it is a thin tightly coiled wire.
- Various studs, stones and pearl, round & *katori* sequins, glass and plastic beads.

Initially, the embroidery was done with pure silver wires and real gold leaves. However, today, craftsmen make use of a combination of copper wire, with a golden or silver polish, and a silk thread. This is because there is hardly any availability of gold/silver on such a large scale as before. Plastic zari threads are also widely used today in different colours.

Embroidery process: For transferring the design on fabric, the motif was first sketched on a thick paper. Its outlines are perforated with a needle and placed over the cloth. Finely powdered charcoal tied in a muslin cloth is passed over the design. Today this transferring is done with a solution of chalk and kerosene oil. Zardozi embroidery is hand stitched predominately by Muslim men. The zardozi craftsmen sit cross-legged around the *adda* – the wooden framework and with the tools of their trade like curved hooks and needles. The fabric is then stretched over the wooden frame and the embroidery work begins.

Stitches: Gold and silver embroidery can be easily done on satin, tissue, velvet, crepe, silk, cotton and net fabric. The motifs are floral and are of Persian influence. Couching, satin stitch, chain stitch, stem stitch and running stitch are the common stitches for gold and silver embroidery. The chain stitch resembles Kutch work and is most commonly used. The stem stitch and the running stitch are used for a miscellaneous type of work. The couching stitch is also very important.

Sometimes certain parts of the designs like leaves and flower patels may first be padded with coarse threads to raise them considerable over the surface of fabric before finally gold embroidered. This is called real bharatkam of India.

Motifs: in zardozi work patterns and motifs are influenced with Persian craft. Mainly floral motifs are used in this work. Creepers are also form main element of designs. some famous motifs of zardozi are *zaminposh- patti wali buti, khanposh,-champa ki bel, teele wali jail, saazposh-guldauiii buti, asmangir-trees,* stylized flowers, galloping stags, peacocks and running lions.

Products: Earlier zardozi embroidery was done on wearable garments and furnishing and bedspreads mainly for royal families. Nowadays, clothes with zardozi are an integral part for any wedding or important functions as it depicts royalty. Apart from wearable garments, zardozi is also done on cushion covers, table cloths, wall hangings, fabric purses, etc. This embroidery is a costly affair.

KAMDHANI AND FARDI KA KAAM FROM LUCKNOW

Both kamdhani and fardi ka kaam are flattened wire embroidery on thin fabric. In kamdani the wire is worked into motifs whereas fardi, literally dots, uses the same wire to embroider silver and golden dots placed in patterns. The hazara butti, thousand dots design in fardi is characteristic of Lucknow. The zardozi of Lucknow is of a fine variety. The embroidery is called mukaish in Punjab and badla in Gujarat and Mumbai. In kamdani, the wire attached to a small length of thread is pulled through the fabric with a needle. In fardi the wire is used as a needle. For openwork, the fabric is pierced with a porcupine quill or pointed sticks made of ivory, wood or bone. The fabric is laid flat on a blanket and rubbed over with a *cowrie* shell. This flattens and burnishes the wire. The motifs are transferred from a perforated paper stencil. Pattern making is a specialized activity. Kamdani is fast becoming a rarity and most of the craftsmen are elderly men. Fardi ka kaam is done by women in their homes.

ZARDOZI FROM VARANASI AND BAREILLY

The Zardozi craftsmen in Varanasi and Bareilly specialize in embroidering badges and ceremonial robes. Zardozi work on badges is a very exacting craft as the logo specified must be reproduced precisely. Only the best craftsmen in a *karkhana* embroider badges. The metal purls used for badges are commissioned by the Army, Navy and other institutes. The badges are made on small, one-man *adda* (wooden frames). The fabric is felt, velvet or heavy satin. Varanasi specializes in zardozi on emblems crests and borders. Wire purls are couched onto the fabric with needle and thread. The work has a combination of ari and zardozi work. In Mughal India, zardozi adorned court costumes, furnishing, scabbards and trappings of elephants and horses, in Varanasi.

Zardozi in Agra is traditionally done on velvet which is said to have been introduced by the Portuguese. Zardozi flourished in Bhopal for around 300 years. Some of the popular motifs included paan, a name derived from its similarity to the *paan* leaf, flower, *patti* (leaf) and *pachni* (V-shaped motif with zari filled on the inner side).

ZARDOZI EMBROIDERY MOTIFS

Border Design

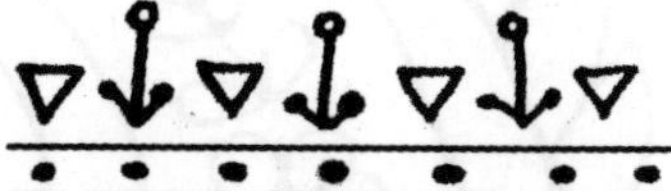

Border Designs

Border Designs

CHAPTER 13

Banjara Embroidery

The liveliest, banjara tribe practice a distinct style of embroidery popularly known as 'Banjara embroidery. Banjara embroidery is very colourful and vibrant and noted for its lively decoration. Banjara tribes are very well-known for their colourful dress and magnificent jewelry, in view of the fact that they wear all their wealth. They preserved their colourful, distinctive heritage of lyricism, songs, poetry, dance, and also maintained a unique aesthetic in their embroidery. The traditional craft has been handed from generation to generation. Banjara women always wear their finest cloths and jewelry, even when doing hard manual labor on building sites.

STORY OF BANJARA EMBROIDERY

The banjaras are a nomadic tribe, believed to be descended from the original Aryan Roma gypsies of Europe. These gypsies migrated through Central Asia and Afghanistan, to settle in the deserts of Rajasthan.

In the prehistoric time, it is likely that they were ironsmiths. They continued to service the agricultural communities by manufacturing and repairing agricultural implements. They also worked as ferries, the makers of the horse shoes and thus came into contact with the armies on the move and became a part of their transportation team. The banjaras were also builders of great monuments. Their nomadic lifestyle led them to spread across India, from Kashmir to Tamil Nadu, from Orissa to Gujarat, spilling over into Sind, Pakistan, Iran and further west. The Banjaras, Vanjaras, Gaudolia Lohars, Lambadas, Vagaries have a common linked tradition.

The Banjara tribe largely settled in Jodhpur and Jaisalmer desert areas of Rajasthan Tamil nadu, Madhya Pradesh and adjoining areas in Maharashtra and Karnataka. Today, they live in small villages called *'tandas'*, settlements on the fringes of towns. The banjaras were known by different names in different parts. In Karnataka, banjaras came to be known as Lambadas or Lambanis. It is believed that the Lambanis came to the Deccan in the 14th century, transporting possessions for Aurangazeb's army. They were suppliers of grain and cattle to the British.

Raw Material: embroidery is primarily worked on a handloom fabric base naturally dyed with many plants and mineral dyes, which banjaras extract. The fabric is mainly cotton. Sometimes wool and silk is used. A multilayer fabric base is prepared by sewing it together, for some specific articles. Silver, brass, gold, cowries, ivory, animal bone, mirrors, coins, cotton and woolen tassels with glass beads are used to adorn banjara textiles and garments. Cowries are very auspicious as they represent Lakshmi, the goddess of prosperity.

Motifs: Designs, motifs and colours were inspired by images from their nomadic lifestyle and their folk traditions and rituals. Striking bold squares, triangles, circles and irregular shapes defined in brilliant contrasting colours forms the distinct patterns of this embroidery. They also outline their motifs with different colour. Red, green, yellow, black and blue are traditionally used colours in banjara embroidery.

Stitches: Needlework is a combination of pattern darning, embroidery stitches, mirror work and appliqué techniques. The embroidery stitches mainly used are running, long and short, interlacing, cross, chain, stem, herringbone and couching. Many local names are given to variations of these basic stitches. There are around 30 to 40 different types of stitches and some of them are:

1. **Vele:** *Vele* is the name for chain stitch. Parallel lines of chain stitch are done to fill spaces and completely cover the base cloth.
2. **Doranaaki:** It is running stitch which is evenly spaced to look like elongated dots.
3. **Kalchi:** *Doranaaki* is first done. Then a thread is intertwined in the dots to form horizontal patterns. The pattern depends on the number of parallel lines made with the dots.
4. **Chukkaler Muggu:** *Doranaaki* is done with a limited number of required dots. Then motifs of geometric flower patterns are interwoven are very similar to the *rangoli* or floor decorations made *by* women in front of their home.
5. **Champa:** Made along the edge of a garment with a narrow strip of material folded into a series of triangles.
6. **Muggu:** in all Indian homes decorative motifs are *drawn* in front of the threshold. For auspicious occasions they are of elaborate design and otherwise simple. The lambadas use these motifs in their embroidery. Dots are evenly spaced and a line is sewed around them in vele.
7. **Maali Kanth:** This is what is generally called herringbone stitch. It is done in a single or multiple lines.
8. **Bakhiya:** It is the back stitch.
9. **Gaddar:** Small rectangular blocks of satin stitch done in one or three colours to form triangular patterns.
10. **Teka:** Consist of small stitches which cross each other at the end of stitch.
11. **Jhinjhini:** Vele done to form triangles and a base line.
12. **Khilad:** It is buttonhole stitch used for edging.

13. **Muggu phool:** A flower of eight patels outlined with vele.

Products: The Banjara women wear *Pheti (gaghras), Kanchali or kaalli (cholis)* and *Chatiya (odhnis)* in bold appliqué and mirror work. They also embroider purses for money or areca nuts *and* square tasseled *rumals* edged with cowries, which are used for presentations at ceremonies and in dances.

Initially, banjara embroidery was restricted to the traditional wears of the women of the community but nowadays, embroidery is found on a number of items like bags, belts, bed spreads and wall hangings, cushion covers, sofa backs etc.

Traditional embroidered products:

- **Kothala:** Kothala or Kotli is the single most important ceremonial textile amongst all banjaras. It is a square embroidered piece measures approximately 50 cm. It has many uses. It can be folded in a number of ways to make different kinds of elaborate bags, shaped like a large envelope used to hold all the smaller dowry pieces. This bag is almost embroidered all over with *bakia,* a kind of back stitch. The corners have cowries (shells) and *phoonda* (pom-pom made of coloured threads or goat's wool). This can also be used as water pot cover.
- **Gala-Phulia:** It is a pot holder, traditionally used by women to carry pots on their heads. It has 3 pieces; the ring or *indhoni,* to hold the pot, the square flap put on the ring and the rectangular piece that is hang down from the base of the pot to the base of the neck. The rectangular piece is most elaborately embroidered with a stitch called *gadri* and mirrors. The edges are lined closely with cowries as also often the centre piece.
- **Gano:** This is a square piece of cloth used to cover the pots on ceremonial occasions. This is done with patchwork, red in the middle and blue in borders. Sometimes borders are divided in half in which one is red and the other is blue. Corner pieces are of the opposite colour to the middle piece.

- **Chandiya:** this beautiful embroidered piece is used for decorating the face of a cow gifted as a dowry to the groom at the wedding.
- **Dhavalo, or Ceremonial Square:** it is the most important type of ceremonial textile called as Dhavalo with reference to Dhavalo songs, prayers undertaken by the new Banjara bride. It is folded into different sorts of bags. Typically it is decorated with cowry shells, and utilizes a combination of flat and crossed stitches. It measures about 50 cms square. The centre panel clearly illustrates embroidery that fully covers the background cloth, using primarily flat stitches. This work is best known of banjaras found in North Maharashtra, Northeast Karnataka and Andhra Pradesh.
- **Man's wedding bag:** A traditional small square four-pocketed wedding bag.

The nomadic banjara community of Rajasthan creates beautiful embellishments on cloth. The banjara women make symmetrical embroidery by lifting the warp thread of the fabric with a fine needle and making triangles, diamonds and lozenges, parallel to the weft thread, giving the effect of an extra weft weave. They specialize in making borders of long skirts. The base cloth is usually handwoven madder (red-coloured cloth), over which embroidery is done in yellow, green, red , off-white and black. *Cowrie* shells and tassels are also use with the embroidery.

BANJARA EMBROIDERY MOTIFS

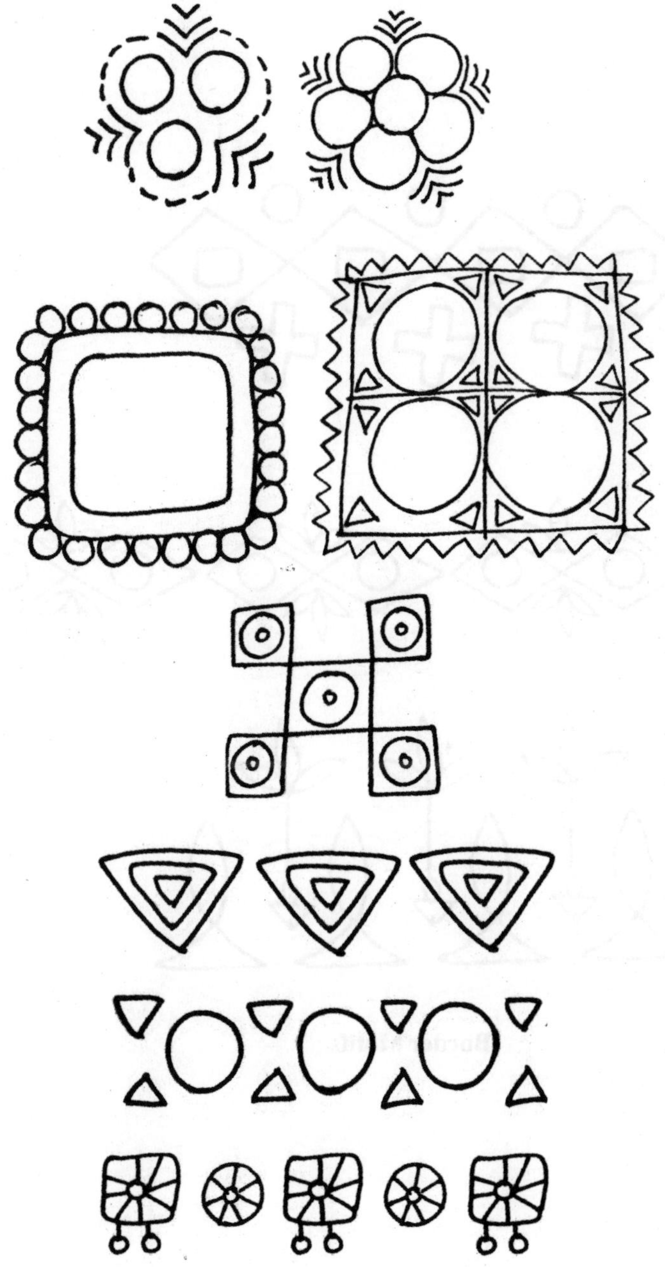

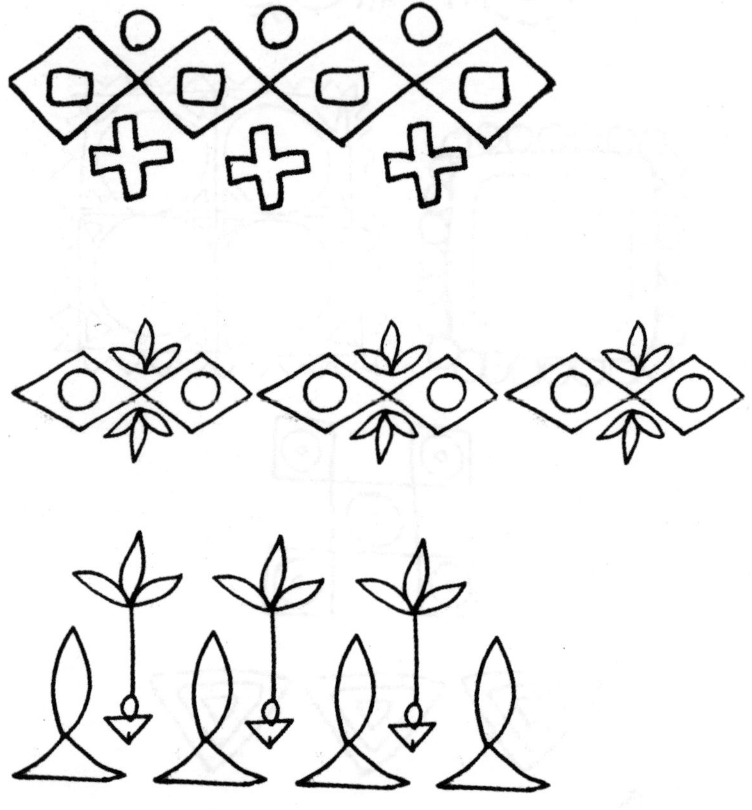

Border Motifs

CHAPTER

14

Embroidery of the Toda Tribe

In India, there are various embroidery forms peculiar to each state. Toda embroidery of Tamil Nadu is one of them. The southern part of Tamil Nadu is surrounded by very beautiful Nilgiri hills popularly known as Ooty. Nilgiris is the abode of many interesting tribes- Todas, Kotas, Kurumbas, Irulas, Mullukurumbas and Paniyans. Todas or todu are the prominent one and mostly involved in agriculture and buffalo rearing. The todas are believed to be of Greek origin.

Story of Toda Embroidery

The Todu community, have developed their own distinctive style of embroidery called pugur, which means flower. The toda women embroider exclusive shawls employing 'pugur' embroidery. These embroidered shawls are called 'poothkuli' in local language. These shawls were believed to be worn in Greek fashion by both men and women of the tribe. This embroidery is carried out from one generation to other generation.

The origin of todas is shrouded in mystery. It is believed that toda tribes were migrated from the tracts of Central Asia, penetrating India, probably through Baluchistan, 3000 to 4000 years ago. Toda people live in small villages called "*mund*".

Fabric: The base material, normally white in colour, is hand woven unbleached cotton in a balanced weave structure. This particular shawl has three alternate red and black woven stripes at the gap of six inches. The women embroider in between these bands creating a striking *'pallav'*.

Colours: Colour of the ground fabric is off- white. The colours of the threads are red and black.

Stitches: The darning stitch is used for embroidering motifs and patterns. The embroidery is so fine that it looks like weaving. The embroidery is worked on the reverse of the fabric by counting the threads. Thus, the embroidery is reversible. Todas use the rougher under side of the fabric as the right side. While formerly vegetable fibre was used as threads, now embroidery threads are used.

Motifs: Basically all the traditional embroidery inspiration is taken from nature, day to day life activities, and mythological stories and reflects the colours of flora and fauna of that particular region. In this case also the motifs are inspired from local surrounding.

The most important motif is the buffalo horn as the Todas worship the buffalo. Other motifs used are Izhadvinpuguti (a motif named after their priest), *mettvi kanpugur* (a box), *quaint* motif (named after a girl who slipped and fell off the cliff), Sun, Moon, stars, flowers, snakes and rabbit. The geometric motifs, merging with the woven bands are often mistaken for woven patterns.

The women create the design without tracing the pattern and without referring to a book. The embroidery, on the shawl, which is done on the left of the black stripe (around the two red stripes) is called the *karnol*, while the embroidered pattern on the right is called the karthal.

The poothukuli is worn by the todas during their festivals and funerals. The Toda bride and groom drape themselves with the embroidered garment during weddings. The wedding guests too have to wear 'poothukuli' embroidered fabric during the wedding. The embroidery, which intended for funeral, is usually the most elaborate of all.

The poothukuly is not an ordinary shawl. It consists of two five meter lengths of fabrics, embroidered with similar patterns and joined together lengthwise to increase the width of the shawl. Tucked in between the fold of cloth is a pocket that is used to store valuables. To wear, it is folded in half for warmth. It is wrapped around the back covering the left shoulder, held under the right arm and then slung over the left shoulder. The sections that are visible along the shoulders & back are usually richly embroidered.

Contemporary Use

Embroidery of Tamil Nadu has attained appreciation in the national and international market because of its intricate work and exclusive designs. Today, along with the famous toda shawls, the women make other products like bags and bed covers, *dupattas* and table cloth, stoles, *kurtis, pyjamas,* skirts, pants, *salwar-kurta* etc.

Other Embroideries of Tamil Nadu

The Ari embroidery of Tamil Nadu is also famous and widely admired in the international market in Nigeria. The embroidered clothes decorated with *'tikris'* and beads are used by the women of Nigeria during ceremonial occasions. Sri Perumbpadur region of Tamil Nadu is noted for this embroidery work where it is done on sarees and handkerchiefs. This type of embroidery needs to use a frame of wooden beams. The fabric is worked upon with a long needle, threads, *'tikris'* and beads.

Apart from these embroidery works, Tamil Nadu is also known for the 'jaali' or net embroidery work. This type of embroidery work is done with geometric or floral patterns by pulling the warp and weft threads and fixing them with minute buttonhole stitches.

TODA EMBROIDERY MOTIFS

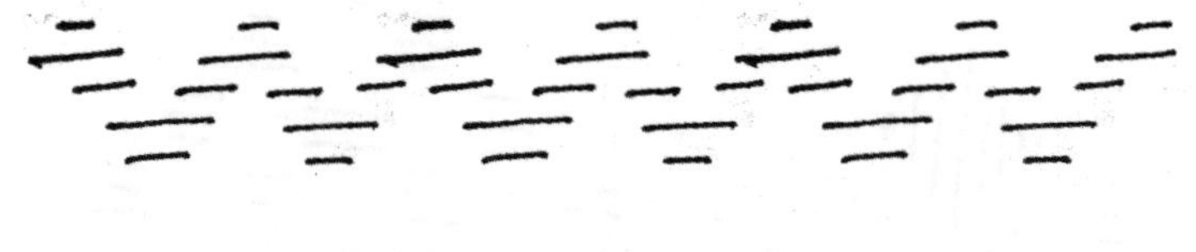

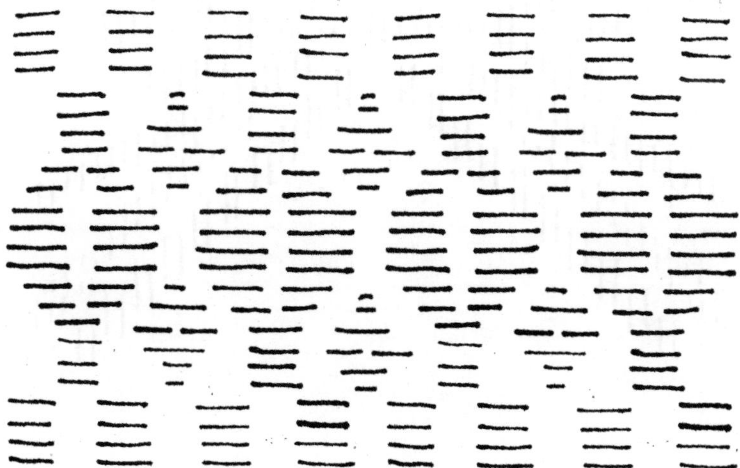

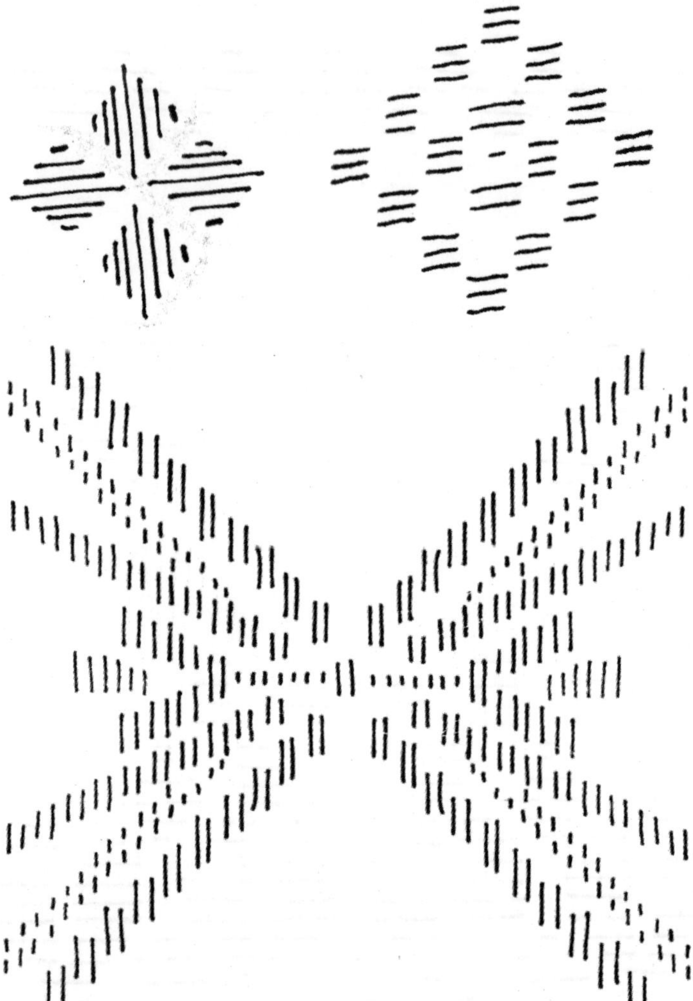

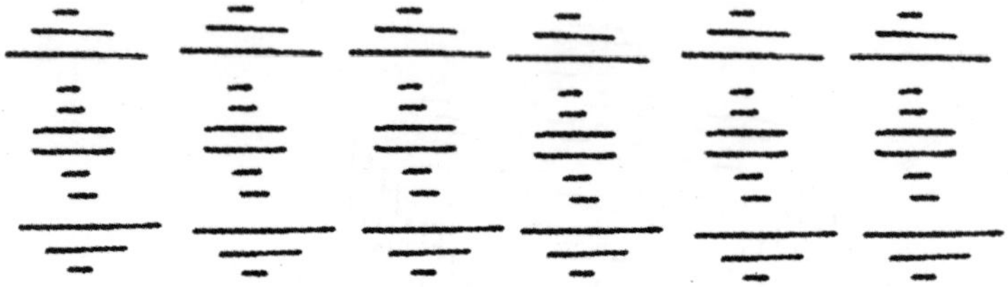

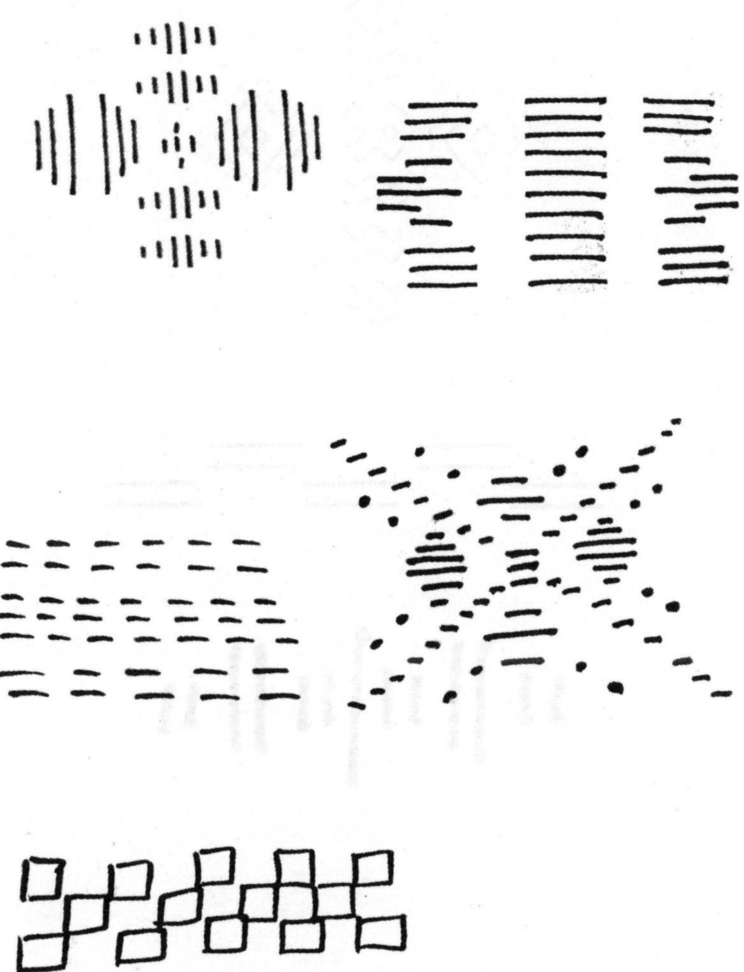

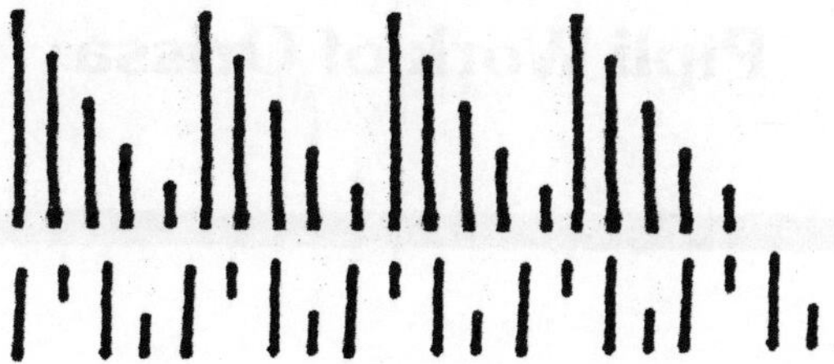

CHAPTER 15

Pipli Work of Orissa

The applique craft of Pipli village of Orissa is distinct in style and imagination. In Orissa, appliqué craft is practiced in Puri, Khallikote, Ganjam and Baudh districts, but Pipli is the principal center. Ganjam district specializes in combining appliqué craft with embroidery.

STORY OF PIPLI CRAFT

The pipli applique work is a vivid expression of Orissa crafts. It is generally accepted that appliqué works of Orissa date back to more than 850 years. Applique in Orissa was basically done by a clan of professional tailors called *'darjis'*. It began as a small scale home craft involving all the family members. Then the *Maharaja* of Puri engaged craftsmen *'sebaks'* to prepare articles for the festivals in the Puri Jagannath temple and set up village Pipli for them to live in. They were especially skilled in designing canopies that is used to cover the chariots during Rath Yatra of Lord Jagannath sister Subhadra and Brother Balbhadra. These canopies are a representation of the beautiful craft of applique and patch work of Orissa. Almost all the family members get involved in this craft.

Technique: The craftsman first prepares the base material in the required shape- square, rectangle, circle or oval, which forms the background for the pieces of art. Appliqué motifs in contrasting colours are then cut in the desired shapes. If more than one of the same cut motifs are required, a stencil is used. These specially prepared motifs are then stitched on a base cloth in predetermined layout and sequence. The actual grace of appliqué craft lies in its intricate stitches namely, *bakhia, guntha, turpa, chikan* and other very delicate embroidery techniques. Raised motifs are prepared by giving several folds. The edges of the motifs are then turned in and skillfully stitched onto the base cloth or stitched by embroidery or without turning as necessary. Nowadays, small mirrors and bright metal pieces are used to enhance its beauty. After attaching the appliqué patches to the base cloth, borders are stitched. The motifs may be coloured or white. The base cloth is usually coloured. In heavy canopies, the base cloth is additionally supported with a back cloth for strength.

Motifs: Temples and other religious institutions extensively patronized this art. The basic inspiration for the art was mainly religious in nature. Stylized representation of flora & fauna as well as few mythological figures are used as common motifs. Major motifs include:

- **Flowers:** *malli* (jasmine), *padma* (lotus) and *suryamukhi* (sunflower), creeper, tree
- **Birds:** peacock, *gandharv, bhairav*, parrot, swan, duck
- **Animals:** elephant, lion, horse, camel, fish etc.
- **Human figures:** lady in skirt and blouse, soldier, king or queen
- **Mythological**: gods and goddesses, Surya , moon and Rahu
- **Geometrical motifs** for borders

The central lotus motif is distinctive of Orissa applique, constructed with concentric rows of triangles, tips of which are filled with cotton, giving the petals an extra dimension. The layout of various motifs and patterns vary according to the shape of the piece. The canopy has a large centre piece which may be a square. This centre piece is then bounded by several borders of different widths. There are appliqué mythical motifs like Rahu, Chandra as well as motifs from nature like flowers etc. In the umbrella or *Chhati* the inner field is arranged in circles, each circle having patches of one motif placed side by side. The layout for covers for horses consists of a series of concentric strips in the portion which covers the neck, each strip having patches of one motif, while the portions which fall on either side of the body are plain, having border all round with or without a motif at the centre of the plain field.

Colours: The Pipli art form typically uses four basic colours - red, white, black and yellow to produce a striking effect. In recent years, green too has been applied vigorously to energizing the craft even more. The motifs used are fairly varied yet fixed. The creative urge of the craftsmen are released in various combination of motifs as well in the mixing of these limited colours.

As per tradition, the colour scheme of the three covers used during the Ratha Yatra is predetermined. The chariot of Balabhadra known as Taladhawaja has a cloth covering of bright green and red, while that of Subhadra known as Padmadhwaja has a cover of bright red and black. The chariot of Lord Jagannath called Nadighosha has a cover of bright red and yellow.

Stitches: The stitching technique varies from item to item and come under six broad categories namely *bakhia, taropa, ganthi, chikana*, button-hole and running. Sometimes embroidered patterns are also used and in a few items mirror work is also incorporated.

1. **Bakhaia:** Simple running stitch used for keeping the patches in position temporarily on the base cloth.
2. **Taropa /Tarupa stitch**: Simple hemming stitch used to stitching appliqué patches on the base cloth where the edges of the patches are turned in and then stitched.

3. **Ganthi stitch:** Similar to blanket stitch used for attractive embroidered motifs.
4. **Chikana stitch:** Chain stitch popular in appliqué work. It is used for binding the edges of the appliqué patch without turning, making textural and ornamental effects on motifs.
5. **Buttonholes**: Similar to blanket stitch although the needle is inserted from outer edge. It is used in making *mudias* (rings) for fixing round-shaped small mirrors for decoration.
6. **Running stitch:** Used for gathering a strip of cloth to make an appliqué motif like *malli*.

Products: The applique items are mainly used during processions of the deities in their various ritual outings. These traditional items are canopies (*chanduas*), big umbrella with long wooden handle (*Chhati*) and heart-shaped wooden piece covered by applique cloth (*Tarasa*). However, the applique work in its best colourful form is most prominent in the cloth covers of the three chariots of the presiding deities during the *Ratha Yatra.*

Seats and pillows in applique are also made for ceremonial use by the deities during the annual ritual of bathing festival (*Snana Jatra*) and are locally known as *'Chakada Kama'* with motifs of 27 stars and geometrical forms. Applique cover is also made for caparisoning the dummy horses in the 'Horse Dance' during *Chaitra* Festival in Puri and other places. *'Jhalar'* another popular item is a sort of frill which is used as a border to canopies and also independently used as decorative pieces.

An interesting and popular item is *'batua'*, a unique Orissan cloth pouch of semi-circular shape with the top being straight. Various layers of cloth forms pockets for storing different items of use like betel leaf, areca nut, lime, etc., as well as for keeping money. Other traditional items like 'Sujnis' or embroidered quilts and *pasa-palli* or the dice-mat were also quite popular.

The process of making the products has remained unchanged over the past few centuries. However during the last two to three decades, both the appliqué products and their style have undergone a tremendous change. The contemporary products include lamp shades, garden and beach umbrellas, kitchen accessories, bed and table linen, wall hangings, handbags and other furnishing items.

TRADITIONAL PIPLI MOTIFS

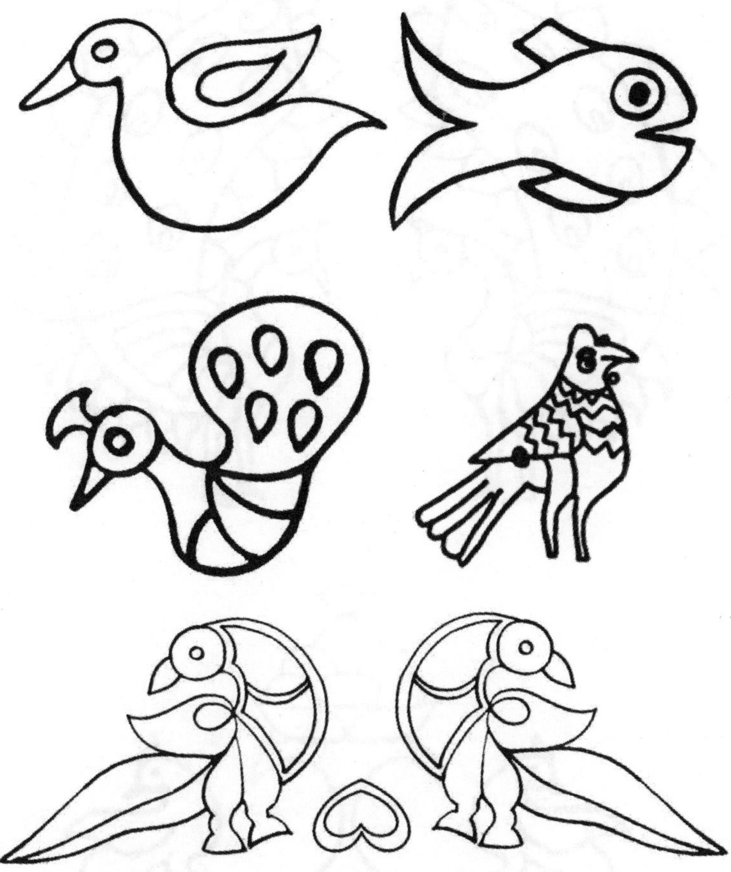

Lord Jagannath with Subhadra and Balbhadra

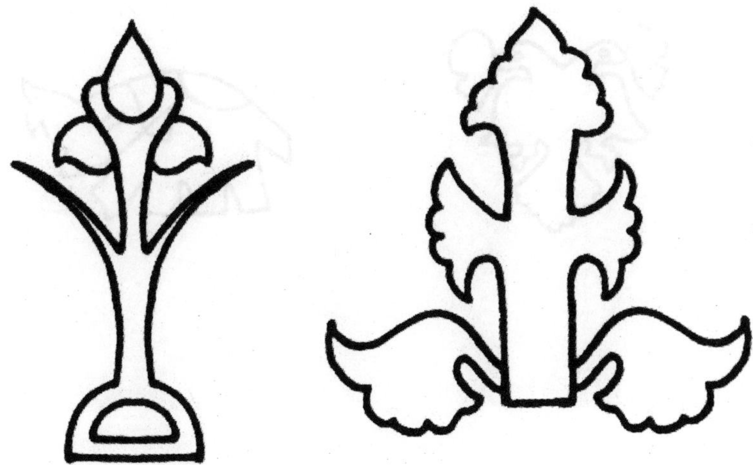

CHAPTER 16

Phul Patti Work of Uttar Pradesh

Phool Patti work is a traditional appliqué embroidery style from Uttar Pradesh, India. Phool Patti work originated from Aligarh district of Uttar Pradesh and is also referred to as "Aligarh Phool Patti work". The embroidery is distinctive of the state and Rampur is the only other location in India where this work is practiced. Thousands of women living in different parts of Aligarh and Rampur are involved in phool-patti work. Men however are sometimes involved in marketing and helping their artisan wives.

Story of Phool Patti Work

Phool-Patti is a delicate form of appliqué work, dating back to the Mughal period. It is believed that phool-patti work, part of the court embroideries, was initially done on *shalukas* (blouses) worn by the begums of Nawabs. The embroiderers were the "*mughlanis*" or housemaids working at the royal courts. The need for embellishment and the hot summer weather are said to have given birth to this embroidery. There is also reference to appliqué *shamiana* or tents from Aligarh in the days of nobility.

Raw material and Technique: In this needlework technique, very small pieces of fine cotton fabric are cut by hand and dexterously folded and shaped into tiny petals, leaves and other geometrical and floral shapes. These are then appliquéd on to the base cotton fabric to create a variety of intricate patterns. Stems are embroidered in 'stem' stitch. The entire embroidery is done by hand including the finish of edges and joining of the seams.

Motifs: The embroidery reflects Persian influence and draws on *mughal* art and architecture designs. The embroidery motifs are in the shape of flower petals or leaves. "Phool" means "flower" and "Patti" means "leaf". Artisans sought inspiration from the natural surroundings like the beauty of flowers, leaves and fruits such as rose, lotus, grapes, mango, melon seeds, grains, others. Some dominant motifs are five and three petal flowers, branches and stems with leaves, tendrils, creepers, paisleys, bunches of grapes and others. In accordance with the Islamic tradition, human and animal figures are avoided.

Colours: This very beautiful embroidery is done using fresh and light colours often shades of pink, red, orange, green, yellow, and tints of blue, to provide a natural look. This refreshing colours' embroidery creates best summer wears for the people of Uttar Pradesh.

Products: The pool-patti work is widely used on women apparels like saari, dupattas and kurti and salwar. Today, for product diversification this work is also performed on georgette and chiffon fabric with unique colour combinations. Small sequins are also inserted in patches of leafs of the flowers.

TRADITIONAL PHUL PATTI MOTIFS

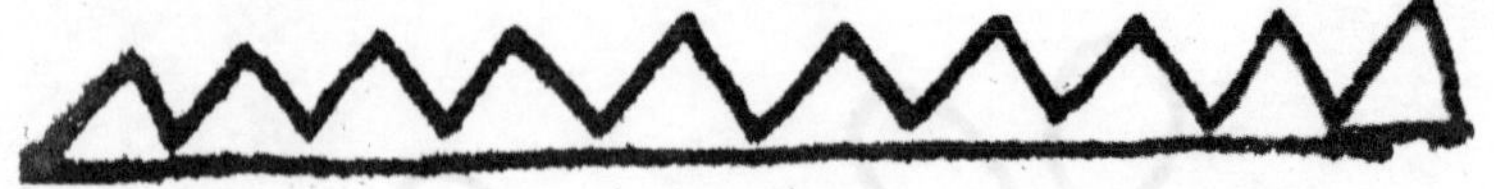

CHAPTER 17
Miscellaneous Needlecrafts

THARU APPLIQUE

The Tharu women from remote villages of Lakhimpur Kheri, Uttar Pradesh, use applique to ornament their traditional garments *ghaghra-choli*, men's caps, jackets and pouches. In this type of applique, incisions are made on the top fabric that is hemmed down on to base fabric. Thus the form is revealed in the reverse. Shapes are not cut out from the fabric as is the case with most appliques. The background fabric is darker than the colour of the applique and the appliquéd layer covers the surface extensively. The patterns are rectilinear and geometric comprising triangles, fine lines and colourful borders. The fabric is bought from wandering salesmen and bright colours are preferred.

LEATHER EMBROIDERY OF CHAMBA

According to a local myth, leather shoes were introduced in Chamba valley, Himachal Pradesh, by a Kangra princess who married into the royal family of Chamba and brought along a cobbler family as part of her dowry. Even today, families of cobblers make slippers of embroidered leather. Slippers are constructed with sheep or goat leather by the male members of this community while the women embroider elaborate felt uppers that are mounted on the leather slippers. Chain stitch embroidery is done with a hooked needle to create stylized flowers and leaves patterns. These are usually embroidered in silk threads and zari threads are also used for further embellishment. The colour palette generally consists of shades of pink, deep green, red, sky blue and yellow, executed on a background of black or maroon. A unique pair of leather shoes with zari belonging to royal family of Chamba is preserved in Bhuri Singh Museum. Leather embroidered belts are also commonly worn by the local people.

MUTHANGI-PEARLSTUDDED ATTIRE

Muthangi denotes special garments and accessories made for the temple deity which were earlier studded with pearls, precious stones and zari. "Muthi" means Pearl and "Angi" means Garment. They are used during festivals to dress the idols. Inexpensive alternatives such as beads are used today. Embroidery units are concentrated around the Minakshi temple in Madurai, Orissa. Items like garments and accessories (headdress) are studded with artificial pearls, artificial stones, and zari by stitching them on a cloth base, usually blue velvet.

DONGARIA KONDH TRIBAL EMBROIDERY

Women of the Dongaria Kondh tribe of Orissa embroider a scarf called "kapra gonad" which they wear over a white saree with a red border. This saree is a single length of fabric that is draped around the lower and upper part of the body and complemented with one scarf worn around the waist and the other draped on the chest. The scarf is given as a token of a proposal by an eligible boy to the girl of his choice. It is embroidered by his sisters or by girls for their lovers. The scarf is woven in basket weave by male weavers of the Dom community and subsequently embroidered by the Dongaria women.

APPLIQUE OF MADURAI

There are only a few hereditary craftsmen practicing applique in Thanjavur-Madurai, Tamil Nadu. They are from the Pilamar caste. The applique technique is used to produce decorated cloth used for religious processions of the temples. Felt or velvet material is appliquéd on to a cotton background. The appliqué pattern is then outlined with cotton cords, in addition to outlines done in embroidery stitches. The background colour is usually red on which pieces of cream, green, yellow and black are appliquéd. The main product is the "*Ther silai*" comprising many components which are part of an ensemble for decorating the temple chariot. Costumes for priests are also made. The bustling Madurai market, well known for selling temple related products, is located near the Minakshi temple in Madurai.

Glossary of Local Terms

Aari	– Hooked needle used in embroidery
Abhala	– Small mirrors
Adda	– Wooden frame on which fabric is stretched before embroidery
Angrakhas	– Men upper wear of kurta style used in olden days
Astadala	– Group of eight
Badami	– Almond's shape
Bakhia	– Simple running stitch
Bel	– Trellised border and creeper
Bharat	– Embroidery
Buti or Buta	– Small flower motif
Chaddar	– Rectangle fabric used as bedcover or to cover body
Chakla	– Coverlet
Chand/chandarma	– Moon
Chapkan	– Men royal upper garment
Chaupad	– Dice game
Choga	– Royal gown for men
Choli	– Bodice
Choli	– Women upper to be worn with skirt or saree

Cowrie	– Conch shell
Darshan Dwar	– The gate of a temple through which god can be seen
Doranga	– Made with two colours
Dori	– Thin twisted cord
Do-rookha	– Double sided fabric
Doushala	– Twin shawls
Durrie	– Thick woven bed spreads
Ghagara	– Skirt
Gopis	– Lord Krishna's female freinds
Gota	– Golden woven ribbon
Guldasta	– Flower pot
Hukka	– Smoking device of Indials
Indhoni	– Pot holder to carry water pots on head
Jalis	– Neat regular holes or net
Jhalar	– Fringe
Kalam	– Pen
Kalka	– Mango shaped Indian motif
Kasaba	– Head dress of Indian women
Kasheeda	– Embroidery
Katori	– Small bowl
Khaat	– Wooden square frame
Khaddar	– Thick handspun and hand-woven cotton cloth
Khes	– Rectangle fabric to cover body
Kinari	– Edging
Krishna	– Famous lord of Hindus, India
Krishnalila	– Dance performed by lord Krishna with his companion freinds
Kundan	– White stone used in metal embroidery

Kunj – Grouped
Kurta – Indian women upper garment
Lehenga – Women lower garment like skirt
Mahabharatha – Great Indian epic
Mahal – Court
Malmal/mulmul – Thin muslin cloth
Meenakari – The enamel work on cloths and other items
Mochis – Cobler
Nandi – Sacred bull of lord Shiva
Naquashband/ Nakshaband – Professionals who traces designs on fabric
Nawabs – Royal Muslim kings
Nayak and Naika – Local heroes
Neel – Llue colour used to trace the design having low fastness
Odhni – Women stole
Padma – Lotus flower
Pahari – Of hills
Pallu – Lower draped border of a saree
Paniyari – Women balancing water pots on their heads
Pankhi – Hand fan
Pashmina – Pure wool fibre from Kashmiri goat
Pat – Silk untwisted yarn used in embroidery
Phirans – Women upper shirt
Phool Patti – Flower and leaf
Poncho – Kashmiri traditional women wear
Purana – Indian holy book

Rafoogar – Professionals who do fabric mending
Ramayana – Indian epic
Rath – Chariot
Ratha Yatra – God's journey on chariot
Rumal – Handkerchief
Sadaris – Jackets
Safeda – White chalk power used to trace design
Saree – Six yard draped unstitched cloth used by Indian women
Sarp – Snake
Shamiana – Tents
Shankh – Musical shell
Sherwani – Men royal coat
Shikargah – Embroidered hunting scenes
Shivlinga – Form of lord Shiva
Sitar – Indian musical instrument
Sitara – Sequin used in metal embroidery
Suhag – Symbol of married woman
Surajmujkhi – Sunflower
Surya – Sun
Swastika – Holy symbol of Hindus
Tassar – Wild silk
Thalia – Square plates cover
Thalposh – Large square plates cover
Til – Sesame seeds
Toran – Door panels
Tulsi – Sacred basil plant
Turpa/turpai – Hemming stitch
Zalakdozi – Chain stitch, crewelwork
Zamindars – Landlords

Appendix

LIST OF TEXTILE CRAFTS OF INDIA

Sl.No.	State	Textile Crafts
1	2	3
1.	Jammu & Kashmir	Shawl weaving (pashmina, kani, amli, doranga, dorukha etc) carpet weaving, namda, gabba, kashmiri embroidery
2.	Himachal Pradesh	Shawl weaving, leather embroidery, chamba rumal, pulan jute slippers, kullu cap
3.	Gujarat	Hand embroidery (kutch and kathiawar), appliqué work, bead work, tie and dye, patola, silk weaving, wool weaving, roghan work, zardozi embroidery
4.	Rajasthan	Block printing, embroidery, gota kinari, appliqué, bagru printing, carpet, bandhani, kota saree
5.	Punjab	Phulkari shawls, khes weaving, durrie weaving
6. 7.	Haryana Delhi	Shawl weaving (phulkari) Zardozi embroidery
8.	Uttar Pradesh	Silk brocade, carpet weaving, chikankari embroidery, appliqué, zardozi embroidery

(Contd...)

1	2	3
9.	Uttarakhand	Natural fibre weaving, pichhaura making
10.	Madhya Pradesh	Weaving chanderi, garbhreshmi saree, banjara embroidery, block printing
11.	Bihar	Carpets, kashida embroidery, khatwa, sujini embroidery, printed textiles, silk weaving
12.	West Bengal	Batik paintings, embroidery kantha, baluchar buttedar, ducca muslin
13.	Andhra Pradesh	Kalamkari, ikat weaving, saree weaving (pochampally, gadwall, narayenpett, siddhipet etc.), himroo and mashru weaving, carpets and druggets, cotton durrie weaving , crotchet laces, banjara embriodery
14.	Karnataka	Saree weaving, (mysore sarees, belgaum sarees, ilkal saree, bangalore sarees, shahpur sarees, molkalmuru sarees etc.), kasuti embroidery, druggets, durries and carpets
15.	Orissa	Jute weaving, pipli appliqué, ikat weaving, sambhalpuri saree
16.	Maharashtra	Silk weaving, paithani saree, nagpur saree
17.	Tamil Nadu	Silk saree weaving (kanjeevaram saree, coimbatore, kumbhakonam sarees, tanjore sarees etc.), bhawani durries, applique work, toda embroidery
18.	Kerala	Sarees (kerakudi, kerakal, balrampuram, kusaru), lace making
19.	Sikkim, Meghalaya, Assam, Tripura, Mizoram, Manipur, Nagaland, Arunachal Pradesh	Silk weaving, hand woven fabrics

INDIA MAP

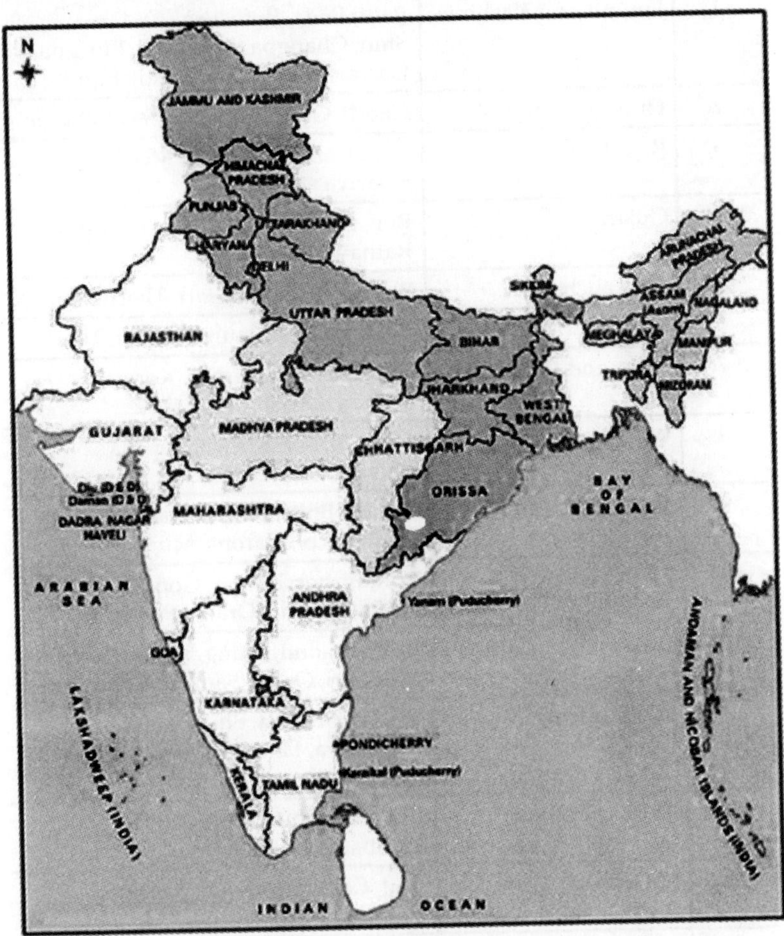
N
JAMMU AND KASHMIR
HIMACHAL PRADESH
PUNJAB
UTTARAKHAND
HARYANA
DELHI
UTTAR PRADESH
RAJASTHAN
BIHAR
SIKKIM
ARUNACHAL PRADESH
ASSAM (Asom)
NAGALAND
MEGHALAYA
MANIPUR
TRIPURA
MIZORAM
JHARKHAND
WEST BENGAL
GUJARAT
MADHYA PRADESH
CHHATTISGARH
ORISSA
BAY OF BENGAL
Diu (D & D)
Daman (D & D)
DADRA NAGAR HAVELI
MAHARASHTRA
ARABIAN SEA
ANDHRA PRADESH
Yanam (Puducherry)
GOA
KARNATAKA
PONDICHERRY
Karaikal (Puducherry)
TAMIL NADU
KERALA
LAKSHADWEEP (INDIA)
ANDAMAN AND NICOBAR ISLANDS (INDIA)
INDIAN OCEAN

LIST OF SOME MAJOR TRIBES OF INDIA

Sl.No.	State	Tribes
1	2	3
1.	Jammu and Kashmir	Balti, Beda, Boto, Brokpa, Dard, Shin, Changpa, Bakarwal, Purigpa, Garra, Mon, Gujjar, Gaddi, Sippi
2.	Himachal Pradesh	Gaddi, Gujjar, Lahuala, Swangla, etc.
3.	Rajasthan	Bhil, Damor, Garasta, Meena, Salariya etc.
4.	Gujarat	Bhil, Dhodia, Gond, Siddi, Bordia, Rathawa, Rabari etc.
5.	Uttaranchal	Bhotia, Buxa, Jaunsari, Tharu, Raji
6.	Uttar Pradesh	Bhotia, Buksa, Jaunsari, Raji, Tharu
7.	Bihar and Jharkhand	Asur, Banjara, Birhor, Korwa, Munda, Oraon, Santhal etc.
8.	West Bengal	Asur, Birhor, Korwa, Lepcha, Munda, Santhal, etc.
9.	Madhya Pradesh	Gonds, Bhils, Baigas, Halba, Panika, Gadba, Kol, Oarons, Murias
10.	Chattisgarh	Bhil, Birhor, Damar, Gond, Kharia, Majhi, Munda, Oraon, Parahi
11.	Orissa	Birhor, Gond, Juang, khond, korua, Mundari, Oraon,Santhal, Tharua, etc.
12.	Maharashtra	Warli, Rathawa, Bhil, Bhunjia, Chodhara, Dhodia, Gond, Kharia, Nayaka, Oraon, Pardhi
13.	Andhra Pradesh	Bhil,Chenchu, Gond, Kondas, Lambadis, Sugalis etc.
14.	Karnataka	Bhil, Chenchu, Goud, Kuruba, Kammara, Kolis, Koya, Mayaka, Toda
15.	Goa	Dhodi, Siddi (Nayaka)
16.	Kerala	Kanis, Uralis, Adiyam, Kammrar, Kondkappus, Malais, Palliyar
17.	Tamil Nadu	Irular, Kammara, Kondakapus, Kota, Mahamalasar,Palleyan,Toda etc.

(Contd...)

1	2	3
18.	Sikkim	Bhutias, Mundas, Lepchas/Rongpa
19.	Assam	Boro, Kachari, Mikir (Karbi), Lalung, Rabha, Dimasa,Hmar, Hajong etc
20.	Meghalaya	Khasi, Jaintia, Garo
21.	Tripura	Chakma, Garo, Khasi, Kuki, Lusai, Liang, Santhal etc.
22.	Mizoram	Chakma, Lusai, Kuki, Garo, Khasi, Jayantia, Mikir etc.
23.	Manipur	Angamt, Hmar, Sema, Maring, Tangkhul, Naga
24.	Nagaland	Konyak, Naga, Kuki, Mikir, Garo, etc.
25.	Arunachal Pradesh	Wancho, Adi, Apatani, Khampi, Miri, Tagin, Dafla, Singpho etc.

Bibliography

Chattopadhyay, K., 1975. Handicrafts of India. Indian Council for Cultural Relations, p. 146.

Chattopadhyay, K., 1985. The Glory of Indian Handicraft. Clarion Books, New Delhi, p. 205.

Crill, R., 1999. Indian Embroidery. Victoria and Albert Museum, p. 144.

Dhamija, J., 2004. Asian Embroidery, Abhinav Publications, p. 343.

Dhamija, J., Bihar Handicrafts. Marg Publications. Bombay, p. 60.

Gillow J. and Barnard N., 1991. Traditional Indian Textile. Thames and Hudson, p. 224.

John I. and Hall M., 1973. Indian Embroideries. Calico Museum of Textiles, p. 222.

Mehta J.R., 1970. Masterpieces of Indian Textile: Handspun-handwoven-traditional. D.B. Taraporevala Sons & Co. Pvt. Ltd. Bombay, p. 56.

Mohanty B.C., 1980. Applique Crafts of Orissa. Calico Museum of Textiles. Ahemedabad, India, p. 25.

Naik, D.S., 1996. Traditional Embroideries of India. A.P.H. Publishing, New Delhi, p. 156.

Paine, S., 2008. Embroidered Textiles: A World Guide to Traditional Patterens. Thames and Hudson, p. 240.

Pandit, S., 1976, Indian Embroidery — Its Variegated Charms. Faculty of Home Science, Baroda.

Shrikant, U., 2005. Ethnic Embroidery of India. Honesty Publishers, p. 143.

Shrikant, U., 2009. Ethnic Embroidery of India, Part II. Honesty Publishers. p. 200.

Thakur U., 1981. Madhubani Paintings. Abhinav Publications, New Delhi, p. 158.

Plates

Toda Embroidery

Toda Embroidered Shawl

Chamba Rumal showing Lord Krishna with Radha having Floral Border

Traditional Chamba Rumal

Traditional Chamba Rumal Showing
Animal and Human Motifs

Traditional Chamba Rumal Showing Rasleela

Chikankari Floral Design

Chikankari: Shadow Work, Jail Work, Murri and Ulti Bukhiya

Gujrati Embroidery

Appliqué Toran from Saurashtra

Chakla: Bead Work Square Hanging from Saurashtra

Patch work from Gujarat

Kantha Showing Animal and Floral Motif

Kantha Showing Human Figure and Lotus Motif in the Centre

Traditional Kantha

Kashmiri Crewel Work on a Robe

Kashmiri Embroideries

Pipli Craft Canopy from Orissa

Pipli Craft

Pipli Craft- Fan

Pipli Craft- wall hangings

Pichwaii from Rajasthan

Pichwaii from Rajasthan

Kasuti Embroidery on a Saree

Kasuti Embridery Motifs

Phulkari Shawl

Phulkari Panchranga from West Punjab

Phulkari from East Punjab

Phulkari in Darning Stitch

Chope Phulkari

Phulkari Shawl

Thirma Bagh from West Punjab

Floral Phulkari Shawl

Darshan Dwar Phulkari

Vari da Bagh

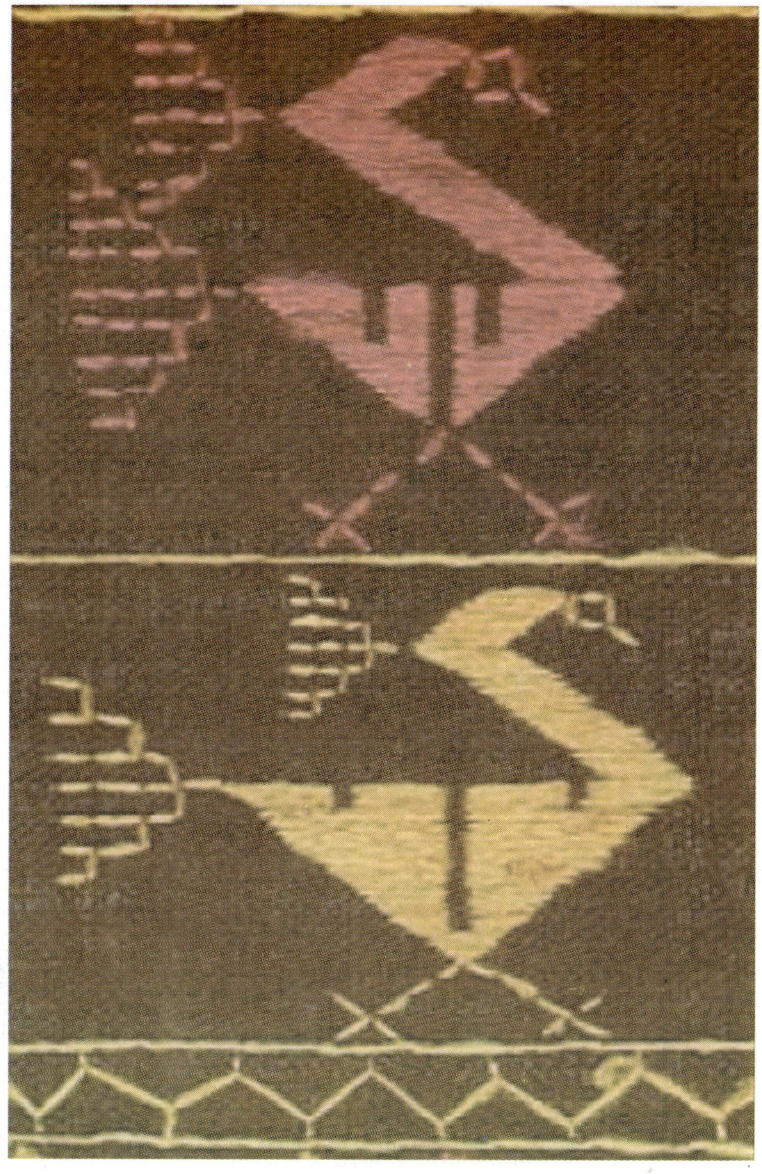

Phulkari from East Punjab

Banjara Embroidery

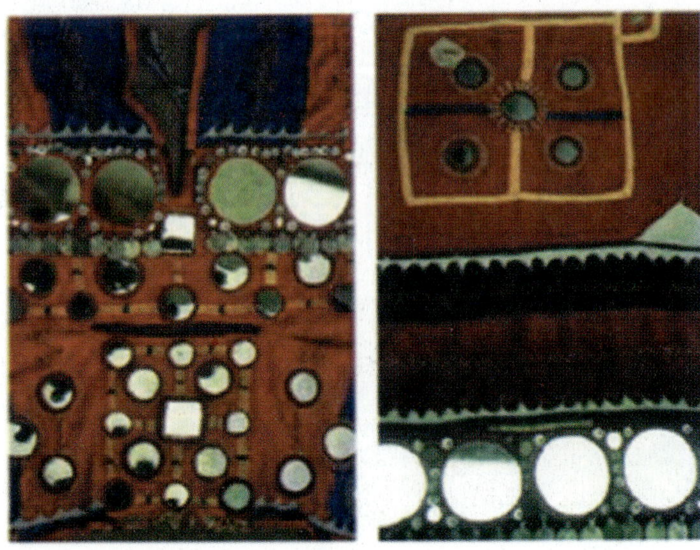

Banjara Embroidery

Banjara Embroidery